AGENDA

Celtic Mists

AGENDA

CONTENTS

INTRODUCTION   5

POEMS

Gillian Clarke:	The Newport Ship	9
	Who Killed the Swan?	10
Liam Ó'Muirthile:	Death Notices – Fógraí Báis	11
	Dung Beetles – Priompalláin	13
Peggy Gallagher:	Ebb and Flow	16
	Aeolian	17
	The Blue Shelf	17
	Landfall	18
Eleanor Hooker:	Mirrored	19
Eamonn Grennan:	Junctures	20
	What Lasts	20
Mary O'Donnell:	Don't Think of Me	21
John Griffin:	Famine Graveyard	22
	The Thought-Desert	23
Ann Joyce Mannion:	At the Headland	24
	Redress	25
Gill McEvoy:	A Glimpse of 'The Essential Brendan'	26
Anne Connolly:	Ground Control	27
Lorna Sherry:	Island	28

Janet Ayachi:	Lavender Gardens	29
	Victor's Women	30
Dan MacIsaac:	Seahorse	31
Gabriel Rosenstock:	Onuphrius (Irish and English versions)	32

ESSAYS

Liam Ó'Muirthile:	Offshore on land: *Poetry in Irish Now*	34
John Griffin:	The Knife of Conscience: The Enduring Value of Patrick Kavanagh's Poetry	44
Eleanor Hooker:	John Hewitt: Ulster Poet	50
W.S. Milne:	The Poetry of Norman MacCaig	55
W.S. Milne:	The Poetry of Alexander Scott	61

POEMS

John F. Deane:	Semibreve	69
	Tuning	70
Sheenagh Pugh:	The Eye	71
Graham Hardie:	A man alone searching for the white narwhale	72
	The Harris Lady	72
Rosalind Hudis:	Ancestral Litany	73
	Cheap Pianos	74
R.V. Bailey:	Tom Tiddler's Ground	75
Robert Stein:	Mette Von O	76
	The Dead	76

Tim Cresswell:	Possible Pubs	77
Mandy Pannett:	Tales from the Sculpture Park	78
William Bedford:	Pillar Box Farm	79
	Sheep-washing	80
Jennifer A. McGowan:	Sounding	81

REVIEW

Ed Weiss:	'Pitch me *vox clamans*': Geoffrey Hill's *Odi Barbare*	83

CHOSEN YOUNG BROADSHEET POET

Richie McCafferty:	*Le voyage dans la lune*	91
	The Weight	91
	En Piste	92
	The Whale	92

NOTES FOR BROADSHEET POETS

Zoe Brigley: Part 2: Social Anatomists — 94

BIOGRAPHIES — 106

Front cover: 'Tory' by Derek Hill.
Courtesy of the Glebe House and Gallery

Illustrations: Carolyn Trant
Pages from Mharbna, an Artist's Book from a residency in Donegal.

Introduction

Welcome to this 'Celtic Mists' issue of *Agenda*. It was originally conceived as an extension to the last 'Retrospectives' issue of *Agenda*. However, it has taken on a character of its own, with makars and bards that speak for themselves.

Neglected poets such as the Northern Irishman, John Hewitt, the Scottish Norman MacCaig, and Alexander Scott are focused upon in enlightening essays by Eleanor Hooker and W.S. Milne. John Griffin throws light on Patrick Kavanagh, a poet honoured in Ireland, but insufficiently known on this side of the Irish Sea.

The essay by Liam Ó'Muirthile, as well as the online essay by Gabriel Rosenstock (excerpts from which appear below) – both poets who write in Irish – show that not only poets writing in minority languages get neglected for multifarious reasons, involving issues such as cultural identity, translation, publication – but that small languages themselves are neglected and even in danger of dying out. Gabriel Rosenstock gives the statistics in his sober look at the state of these languages, according to Unesco's *Atlas of World Languages in Danger* (December 2010):

Cymraeg/Welsh: Vulnerable (611,000)
Gaeilge/Irish: Definitely endangered (80,000 speakers)
Gàidhlig/Scottish: Definitely endangered (58,652 speakers)
Brezhoneg/Breton: Severely endangered (200,000 speakers)
Gaelg/Manx: Critically endangered (revitalised) (1,689 speakers)
Kernewek/Cornish: Critically endangered (revitalised) (2000 speakers)

It is interesting to recall that the Irish language, Ireland's first language, was actually forbidden in Ireland when it was under English rule.

What becomes evident, and vital for the survival, nurturing and flowering, not only of these minority languages but for mainstream languages expressed at their finest in poetry, is the existence of poetry/literary journals such as *Agenda, Poetry Review, Stand, Acumen* and of many smaller grass-roots level magazines such as *Innti* in the Irish language, and those mentioned by Rosenstock:

> After the Second World War, with the establishment of the monthly magazine *Comhar* and the publishing house Sairséal & Dill, new writers came to the fore, in poetry and prose and there are now more books in print than ever before. Long isolated from the rest of the world and with an unacceptable degree of poverty and emigration, Ireland opened up in the 1960s and a youth culture began to assert

itself. This was also an era of civil rights in many places around the world and that movement would be echoed in Ireland, North and South, eventually spilling over into linguistic and cultural rights for Irish speakers who by now were very much a small minority of the total population of the island.

Magazines, broadsheets and pamphlets therefore are vital for the sustenance of a country's living culture. I wish to quote, now, from the beginning of Anne Marie Connolly's interesting essay on the poetry pamphlet in Scotland which appears in full online:

> Poetry is the *uisge beatha* of words-intoxicating, a stimulant, addictive, something to savour and collect and occasionally heading straight for the gutter. No such fate for poetry in Scotland where the flourishing of both the written and the spoken word is evident. With the raw immediacy of poteen a pamphlet has historically caught the passing mood, political nuance, fervent cause. The current world of word-processing facilitates this but many small independent presses with their own flavour and identity are closer to a fine single malt – enduring and distinctive, displaying the maturity of thought which reflects the abiding truths and concerns of us all.

The Gaelige expression for an author becoming publicly known is *tháinig cló*. Seamus Heaney has admitted that 'for many of the best poets now writing it was not only the first means of distribution but the first ratification of their art.' Print first came upon him in a self-stapled pamphlet of eleven poems distributed during the early years of the Belfast International Festival which began at Queen's University in 1963.

At Queen's Hugh MacDiarmid gave a reading of his poems in Scots enthralling a very receptive audience, many of whom were attuned to the strong Scottish influence in their own local accent and idiom. MacDiarmid at seventy was a renowned, controversial and highly influential poet among a thriving 'renaissance' group of Scottish writers all of whom benefitted from the dedicated work of discerning and democratic publishers like Duncan Glen (1933-2008) the founder of *Akros* magazine. Under the *Akros* imprint in 1966 he produced the first of many pamphlets in his prolific career. It was with delight that I lucky-dipped into the first of the green boxes which contain the special archive of pamphlets in the Scottish Poetry Library and found Duncan Glen's own 'This is not a can of beans-a prospect from the window of a small-press publisher' (1999) in which he castigates the mentality of profit, turn-over and lack of risk-taking which underpins the large established firms.

Callum Macdonald MBE was another of those dedicated, independent publishers. He had taken over the production of *Lines Review* magazine a decade previously and so began a long and distinguished career as a printer-publisher who contributed to an invaluable legacy of Scottish culture. He had already been working with many of the same talented men (a notable exclusiveness) as both poets and editors – Hugh MacDiarmid, Sidney Goodsir Smith, Norman MacCaig, Iain Crichton Smith and Sorley MacLean. Many forged life-long friendships and he, through Macdonald Publishers and Printers, ensured that their writing was widely available to all.

Scotland had a well-established tradition of pamphlet publishing but it was through the foresight, imagination and tireless efforts of Tessa Ransford OBE that the Scottish Poetry Library was opened in 1984. She had felt somewhat isolated in her own writing practice and realised that other poets also needed an opportunity to meet regularly to share, discuss and support one another in their work so in 1981 she inaugurated the School of Poets. A dozen like-minded men and women began this stimulating and effective group which still flourishes at the SPL, giving both new and experienced poets the opportunity to gather in a welcoming place and explore their work in a supportive, honest, non-competitive atmosphere. No one teaches and everybody learns. For many it has been the launching pad towards publication.

Agenda gave prominence years back to both Tom Scott and Hugh MacDiarmid who, it seems, were never properly accorded their due. This present editor too, over the years, has placed a great emphasis on Celtic poetry in general issues of the journal and in special issues such as The Irish issue of *Agenda*, guest-edited by Patricia McCarthy at the invitation of William Cookson the founding editor who was then in situ; the John Montague 70th Birthday issue, the Greg Delanty 50th Birthday issue and the special Welsh issue (for availability of these issues see backlist online).

To conclude: let us listen to Gabriel Rosenstock who quotes most relevantly from an essay by Calvino:

> Overambitious projects may be objectionable in many fields, but not in literature. Literature remains alive only if we set ourselves immeasurable goals, far beyond all hope of achievement. Only if poets and writers set themselves tasks that no one else dares imagine will literature continue to have a function …

Let us hope that the 'celtic mists' clear so that all poets and readers can make poetry 'a dance of the intellect among words'.

Patricia McCarthy

Gillian Clarke

The Newport Ship

Tatters of torn sails are gulls drifting
above the long brown muscles of the Usk
where the great ship slept five hundred years, a husk
embalmed in oils of alluvial mud and grit.

Hands that launch her now into the light of day
from the restless wrestling waters of Usk and Severn,
from the silt, the salt, the silence where she lay,
are tender as those who lift a broken man.

Now, just to see her, to imagine, is to hear
the clatter as men lapped planks to build the hull,
rang home the nails; and sailors drawn by the sea's pull
who crossed the unmapped wilderness of fear,

to beach on this shore. Ship without name abandoned
to the heave of tides, the scour of rain and wind,
she gives up her bones again like a queen unbound
from her winding-sheet, robed in sunlight, crowned.

Who Killed the Swan?

'She is mine,' said the river
holding the swan on its palm like a lily.

Said the sky, 'She is mine to have and to hold,
my small white cloud of cold.'

'She is mine,' sighed the wind, wounding the air,
winnowing water, lifting a wing.

'Mine,' said the sun, noosing the swan
with a cold gold ring.

The cob swims in silence, its neck a question,
head downcast over water's mirror.

He lifts archangel wings to scorch the sky,
churning water and wind to rise

above the river, beating alone upstream.
'She is beside me, my soul, my dream,

the current under my heart.
Where I fly, she flies beneath me.'

Liam Ó'Muirthile

Two poems in English and in Irish

Death Notices

There was a time
She would read them aloud
From the newspaper,
Remarking on how we were linked:
Close, not so close, distant
And if there was no blood tie there
'I wonder are we any relation?'
And she'd go into relations by marriage
And acquaintances
Naming people back in time,
The ones that were alive
The ones that were dead
The ones that were married
The ones still living in the country
The ones in the city
A pattern of relations
Spun into her spider's web.

I had escaped all that
Or so I thought
But there's not a day now
When I open the page
Of the death notices
Scanning them
That I don't hear her voice
A live recording
Through the print in homage
To the souls of the dead,
A mother's old-fashioned tone
From my early years,
Incanting.

Translated from the Irish by Gabriel Rosenstock

Fógraí Báis

Bhí tráth
go léadh sí iad os ard
amach as an nuachtán,
ag cur cóngas gaoil isteach
gairid, sínte, i bhfad amach
nó mura raibh gaol fola féin ann
'I wonder are we any relation?'
is ríomhadh sí gaolta cleamhnais
nó lucht aitheantais
ag sloinneadh daoine siar amach,
a oiread acu a bhí beo
a oiread acu a bhí marbh
a oiread acu a phós
a oiread acu fós faoin tuath
a oiread acu sa chathair,
ag fí gréasáin mhuintire
ina líontán damhán alla.

Thugas na cosa liom
mar a cheapas,
ach níl lá anois
go n-osclaím leathanach
na bhfógraí báis
á scanadh,
nach gcloisim a guth
ina thaifeadadh beo
tríd an gcló in ómós
d'anamacha na marbh,
sean-nós máthar is mé óg
á chanadh.

Dung beetles

for Dermot Somers
'...inasmuch as it is almost according
to the fashion of the dung beetle they act,
when writing concerning the Irish.'
     History of Ireland – Geoffrey Keating

No longer a mountain
in the weatherbeaten typeface
of the moor
but the outline of penmanship
against the sky
incorporeal as a dream.

We follow the veins of backroads
away from the highway
into a small world,
as he himself said,
and sunbathe for a while
in Tubber. Birds

as hopelessy intoxicated
in their air-divings
as we are after the mountain
but our bones are reluctant
to brave the shitty path
in the old graveyard;
and yet we do it.

It stands alone
by the wall of a ruined chapel,
the worn trace of carved words
under our fingers
once perfectly chiselled
in the old Gaelic script
for those who could read it.

Still there's much satisfaction
to be derived
from all the shoots
and growth of May
and when she asks
'What insect is it that sings?'
'Cars buzzing past
beyond', I reply. 'Dung beetles'.

Translated from the Irish by Gabriel Rosenstock

Priompalláin

do Dermot Somers
'...ionnus gur b'é nós, beagnach, an phriompalláin
doghníd, ag scríobhadh ar Éireannachaibh...'
                  Foras Feasa ar Éirinn - Séathrún Céitinn

Ní hé an sliabh
faoi aghaidhchló síonchaite
na móna níos mó é,
ach imlíne pheannaireachta
in aghaidh na spéire
agus aerthoirt bhrionglóide ann.

Leanaimid féitheoga cúlbhóithre
i leataoibh ón mótarbhealach
isteach i ndomhan beag,
mar a dúirt sé féin,
is deinimid bolg le gréin
tamall i dTobar. Tá na héin

chomh mór ar meisce
ag déanamh ruathar san aer
is atáimid féin tar éis an tsléibhe,
ach leisce inár gcnámha
cosán bualtraí seanreilige a shiúl;
fós tugaimid faoi.

É ina sheasamh leis féin
le falla fothraigh séipéil,
rian na bhfocal saoirsithe
tréigthe faoi na méireanna,
iad snoite tráth, an té a léifeadh,
i seanchló Gaelach.

Fós bainimid sásamh aerach
as borradh athfháis na Bealtaine,
is nuair a fhiafraíonn sí
'Cén fheithide í sin ag crónán'?
'Gluaisteáin ag scinneadh thart
thall,' a fhreagraím. 'Priompalláin.'

Peggy Gallagher

Ebb and Flow

On the fray of tide
amid sea-wrack and razor-shell
lies the full stretch of your life
          your small body stilled
a bone-work torso
from haunch to delicate forepaw

          sand shifts
  as the rocking waves
unstitch
     your handful of days

     your skull stripped clean
  a christening cup
a receptacle
       the sea enters
          and leaves

     on a ridge of kelp
      and splinter shells
  and the moon
 trawling her wide acres
      gathers you back to her bed.

Aeolian

How easy to make promises,
    don't you know memory is not mortal
        it keeps returning

and the wind is a gossip
    that hoards a swarm of words
        and braided into the wind

are clear ocean sounds
    a yearning we cannot touch,
        or reach for the words.

It is a house foundered,
    a shell-like sound
        that roars with silence.

It is a shoreline half-eaten by waves,
    it is the same yearning that closes us
        opens us again.

The Blue Shelf

Stop looking for what lies behind
the glass mountain, Grandmother said.
But why? if, on a summer's day

the lake flips open a disc
to find Cairn's Hill immersed
head and shoulders in the text

and the trees' sisterly whisperings,
peering down their bell-skirts
at the patina of their peep-toe selves,

their lived space portioned between horizons,
a blank pane that can flex with the sky,
who then would say where Eden lies.

Landfall

When the gale is spent,
when darkness empties,
yields to a brightening scrim,

and a blade of dim brilliance
turns its edge on the horizon
opening a seam in the sea's teal,

a sheet of lit syllables,
a glittering disremembrance
of the night's pitch and heave;

the growing light probes
its salted hallways, its spun foam
white as our ancestors' bones

that roam its lanes and byways
cold and mindless
touching the waves blindly.

But look –
the sea moves her mirrors,
land swims at lit intervals,

steady-keeled, our battered craft,
rank with fish stink and diesel,
slices a wake toward the headland.

An uncontrollable tremor;
light spills through the shoulder
of the limestone shore.

Eleanor Hooker

Mirrored

She visited again last night, no pike this time.
She was singing too. Her song is the sound of a heavy body
Dragging itself, deadly, up the stairs. Her malady
Not too dissimilar to that thud-thump heartbeat
In my ears. She brought mirrors into my mind
And in my mind she filled the mirrors with crows,
Huge-beaked, hungry crows. That fed. And though
I couldn't move, I kept my eyes open,
I wasn't frightened; I knew sooner or later I'd wake,
And she would have to leave with her mirrors and her crows,
Leaving my pulse behind.

Eamonn Grennan

Junctures

One day braided into another plaits the big with the small
       the purple wedge of Duchruach when morning light colours
the pale slate-shaded cloud it wears like a shawl
       with the quick pink tongue the brindle-cat flicks licking
and lapping up the bread and milk he's left out
       or linking a big wind that rattles the sycamore and makes
a rat-scratching in its dry leaves to the nervous click-ticking
       one robin offers air to signal that the hungry cat's about
or setting a cow's huge head drag-snapping and munching
       among the fuchsia branches where two bluetits
are moving shadow-silent and tiny in their enormous world
       or bringing the radiance of noon to rest on the broad lake
as on any single separate-from-everything illuminated blade of grass.

What Lasts

What lasts has to be simple: a map of the old world or a sky
       dark with the passage of starlings or cold growing colder
with the promise of snow or the colours in the old map or
       a stretch of winter-licked grass or grey roads white with salt
or a hawk gliding wide-winged to a naked maple to observe
       his hungry world while a squirrel gives one piteous moan
then falls silent as Master Redtail perched up there peers about
       lifts head sniffs wind *(snow coming)* or how (simple too)
before ceding to snowmist and giving their shapes up to ice
       reeds and trees turned sepia are pasted to parchment air
as ideograms for *so fleet now here all colours look now gone*.

Mary O'Donnell

Don't Think of Me

Don't think of me as having been unkind,
An eyewitness who did not try to speak.
Ever since, dark thoughts parade my mind.

In photographs, perched side by side, I find
Your wary childhood eyes, while mine are meek.
Don't think of me as having been unkind.

The awkward truth is, I was never blind,
I found a secret stream, my way to seek,
Although since then dark thoughts assail my mind:

Child-scrawled problems mailed unsigned
To one who might assuage the silent shriek.
Don't think of me as having been unkind.

We soldiered on, not touching, unaligned,
As other silenced children dared not speak.
Since then, dark thoughts arrest my mind.

The witnessed truth still scourges. Yet we find
Some molecule of peace within what reeks.
Don't think of me as having been unkind.
Ever since, dark thoughts parade my mind.

John Griffin

Famine Graveyard

Down in that field of mulch our feet
cushioned by moss sank into soggy soil.
The Atlantic was just over the next hill
and we could hear it crash
and smell the kelp
and see the promontory beyond.

Here was the last refuge of the dead,
the final plot arable enough
to plant our ancestors –
they're buried here in broken vaults
and slanted headstones where crosses
sink into nameless, sunken graves.

Here lie the serfs that gave us our patronymic,
long dead now in their famished graves,
forgotten by the wintry sea, where skulls
tumble out of ruined crypts
that soon will wear softly away
like the foamy hem of the tardy tide.

Yet you still felt grief here,
enough to hang your head,
and holding onto a tombstone for balance,
you blessed yourself and looked back
to land where these bones eked hardship
from a tableaux of stones.

The Thought-Desert

I have spent my days learning to pour the potion
of my days into draughts of forgetfulness.

That is the desert of last things, of sun-baked minarets
and silent, birdless nests amid the sweltering palms,
of golden tulips burned to veins of nitre and ash,
and of the still and pollenless droughted air.

That is the desert of new beginnings, of ginger
tinctured toasts and the musk of lingering smiles
in the sinless bazaars — all that is alien there but hope
greens the fruited arbors in the oasis of the future.

This is the desert of loss and exile, where hunger goes
to find a heart to eat, but not the garrisoned heart
that boils itself to vapours nor the frozen-fisted heart
that pummels love into vaults of daggered ice.

The desert of cadences calls. It knows the colours of oblivion.
But who will plant a tear in the eye of the sun? Cry no more
for what's evaporated and done, only climb your Qibla wall
by the shimmering phoenix fronds and wait for all the dates to fall.

Ann Joyce Mannion

At the Headland

Foolish to believe you could not exist
outside the frame of that river-field,
the train's clatter over the bridge shivering
those ancient sycamores like a breeze.

Morning falls into the wet silence of the beach.
This ocean. Its endless lanes and alleys opening
and closing and you realise that the waves
curling round your ankles could easily dilute memory.

Their touch startles. You don your new coat,
fit it to your shape, fill its seams with the scent
of meadow-sweet, sew runes as buttons lest you forget.
Your fingers furrow the sand for the sensation of soil.

At the water's edge you discover a new light.
The fired ware of who you are draws you in
to the interplay between sky and sea.
There is a gradual shift in your perspective.

In the quietness place takes possession of you.
The carried ghost of the river field turns to sleep.
Land voices begin to slip down among the rock-pools,
mingle with the calls of gulls singing you
                              into the rocky headland.

Redress

The grandmother begins a new canvas
paints black lines of unequal lengths,
silence marks lifted from her bedroom wall.

She drenches the sky with blue,
adds sunspots where shadows formed.
Indigo dust leaches into her lemon skirt.

Her voice opens like a flower.
Angled words slip from her tongue,
reel into each other, fall into the pigment.

The markings of a road back,
lanes she might have taken,
the hundred bird calls ignored.

She is hunkered down in the marsh pool
hands squelching secrets out of black mud.
shedding sorrow in a slow absolution.

In the distance the song of a meadow pipit,
a fine needle unravelling the pinioned shadows.
From the hollow of her palm brush strokes lift

cover the dark lines hiding her own intimacies.
Slowly her mountain is cleansed of regrets,
that hunger for impossible love slaked.

She falls into trees calling her name,
repeats it as though it was lost in years
and had just been discovered.

Gill McEvoy

A Glimpse of 'The Essential Brendan'

for Brendan Kennelly

His belly pushing
against the limits of the lectern,
his fingers playing excitable rhythms
on its wooden dullness as if
he wanted to turn the lives of poets
dead and gone to music,

willing us to rise up singing
from the brutal benches of the
lecture hall, clap and cheer
to honour the poets' legacy from the past,
celebrate the chain of future,

for even then
his eyes were dancing,
his feet were dancing,
his words were dancing.
His lost father
dancing behind him.

Anne Connolly

Ground control

In a charitable chair I leant forward
as the old pilot throttled back his memory
soared with bluebirds over the white.

We'd both been up there in the skies
hospital bed ditched at the ether's edge
face fired again, controlled, supreme.

Then the ward sister told us of the towers.
Normal was thrown into Dangerous Sharps
to be disposed of with tomorrow.

Since that September day no landing strip
exists to jettison the pay-back-load.
No dementia to wipe the rewind clean.

Lorna Sherry

Island

Space wide and blue,
sea-washed. Cold as the women there
who are narrow. Narrow as the ribbon roads.
Hard as the rocks and as steady.

Space, fresh and blue,
sea-washed, bright and sharp.
Sharp as women's tongues.
Tongues with power and spume.

Janette Ayachi

Lavender Gardens

Seaside trips on the train during summer,
railcards   seagulls   and jelly shoes,
witches in Eastbourne, candy floss in Brighton,
sand matted   in our hair   for days.

The Diary of an Edwardian Lady open on mother's lap
for hours;   African daisies,   strelitzia, tulips,   irises,
slick rodedendrums. She picked and painted
flowers   until winter.
I remember our visit to the Lavender Gardens
the colour and smell asphyxiating, undulating
quarries of lavender engulfed children,
its febrile turbulences of colour marked no escape,
soap and scented   stationary
followed us home   as souvenirs.

What were we supposed to find there
under the tendrils and barnacles   of opiate lavender,
panic attacks amongst the spume,
time away from the   howl and dust
of the underground   to a playground of plants
          scratching our bare legs
we were two young sisters   chasing each other
shins   swiped   with   pollen.

Victor's Women

Your second wife was found
     in Princes Street Gardens, two bottles
          of cheap wine pressed into her blotched hands
fifty-nine paracetamol in her stomach
a plastic bag tied over her head.

The police passed her to the paramedics
     you took her home to her own barbiturate bed
          avoiding grooves in the road like a new father
how fragile she was in the rear-view mirror
wrapped in white counting cars and clouds.

Day after day you watched the cleaners
     underline the street with florescent trails
          life resumed to routine and she continued
to conjure up the women that entered your life
all of them damaged enough to dismantle.

As one female frayed into the background
     you unravelled the following quick-fix affair
          until each reservoir of placebo love ran dry
and they were all left in pieces, placed in a box
with a plastic window, shelved for their next
               puppeteer of pain.

Dan MacIsaac

Seahorse

Hippocampus

Little changeling
staked to your patch
of eelgrass, your
hue shifts with mood.

Mute and homely,
you are fair game,
however your colour
may flux.

Camouflage cannot
free you from
the drag net
scraping along the sand.

Caught, you are
ground up –
a quack cure
for impotence.

If only you could
transmogrify into
myth – the great
sea steed of Poseidon

towering and relentless
as a tidal wave
howling down
on the human shore.

Gabriel Rosenstock

Onuphrius

I am Onuphrius
the voice
the silence of the desert
my only garments
the hair on my body

I was once a woman of rare beauty
then God gave me a beard
in which the breeze of Heaven plays

I am Onuphrius
the sweet words of God sustain me
and quench my thirst

Translated by Gabriel Rosenstock

Onuphrius

Mé Onuphrius
mé guth
mé tost an ghaineamhlaigh
gan d'éadach umam
ach clúmh

Spéirbhean tráth a bhí ionam
gur bhronn Dia féasóg orm
trína séideann leoithne na bhFlaitheas

Mé Onuphrius
briathra milse Dé a chothaíonn mé
is a mhúchann mo thart

Liam Ó'Muirthile

Offshore on land – *Poetry in Irish Now*

If being a poet in Irish feels like living offshore on land, that feeling of offshoreness seems to be the undercurrent of a primary call: of journeying there in order to stay here. A paradox of course, but confirmed and sustained by experience. In the world of poetry in Irish – a compass without co-ordinates – each poet marks out an individual point without making the compass whole.

There have been and are enough poets working in Irish to box the compass – 'to know and to be able to recite the points and quarter points of the magnetic compass from north through south to north again, both clockwise and anticlockwise. It is now a lost art...' *(The Oxford Companion to Ships and the Sea, 2006)*. In Irish now, each recites his or her own point outside the hearing range of the other. A strange journey indeed.

It was still possible in or about 1968, with Seán Ó Ríordáin's poems in *Eireaball Spideoige* (1952), 'Adhlacadh Mo Mháthar' ('My Mother's Burial') and 'Saoirse' ('Freedom') embedded in the Irish language syllabus of secondary-level schools, for poems to have a far-reaching effect on a generation which was entering University. The Irish language itself, as an entity, had a viable currency of thoughtful and coherent expression. Literacy in Irish among a generation of learners was peaking. Literature was still a gateway to the language, with television just gaining a foothold. There was a congruence between education, a first glimpse of economic ease, the community language of the Gaeltacht, and notions of national political aspirations and local cultural identities. The Northern Ireland Troubles were beginning to rock the South to its core. Paris had erupted. World events impinged. Protest was a new religion of the age.

Cork city was to become the main *locus* for the great burst of poetry in Irish through the poetry journal *Innti*. The city had an open backdoor to the southwest and the feeling of being a European crossroads-on-sea. It was possible, even in the late Sixties, to imagine an authentic Irish language voice of the English-speaking city. Nowhere else in Ireland had the written text of the language been worked so late into the nineteenth century by dairy farmers, tradesmen, tailors, stonecutters, teachers, Catholic and some Protestant clergy, and professional scribes with commitment and playfulness, and with an enduring sense of regional and local identity. The remnants of a classical tradition had left their tidal mark. Frank O'Connor too, was a fluent Irish speaker who had mediated the world of poetry in Irish through his translations. All this, the strong oral storytelling and *seanchas*, and much more had contributed to zones of feeling and thinking which could be construed as alternatives to the predominant culture.

The poet Seán Ó Ríordáin shuffled within that nexus, in his forays into the city and in his TB room on its outskirts in Iniscarra. The village of Iniscarra was not only a bus terminal for Sunday afternoon trips to the river Lee, but also a regional symbol of the economic regeneration of Sixties' Ireland. A new hydroelectric dam had been built there. Ó Ríordáin's work reflects that renewal, in the shadows cast by the candlelight at his bedside on his poems, and in his diary references to his brother's hopes for employment on the so-called Lee Scheme.

If we are to believe in any linear descent at all – and it may be doubtful – poetry in Irish became possible for the generation born in the early 1950s and subsequently, when Seán Ó Ríordáin sat in a sunny apple orchard re-reading a letter from his dead mother in the early 1940s. The Aran Island poet Máirtín Ó Direáin (1910-1988), too, had attended a lecture on poetry in Dublin by the scholar and Revivalist Tadhg Torna Ó Donnchadha from Carrignavar, in the late 1930s, which kickstarted his work.

The fact that Ó Ríordáin's mother's letter was in English, and the resulting poem 'Adhlacadh Mo Mháthar' in Irish, is more than an underlying reality. It is integral to all contemporary poetry in the Irish language, which is a poetry of two languages, one on the page, the other crowding the stage. While the dead mother syndrome may be of more enduring interest to psychoanalysts than to poets, nevertheless, Ó Ríordáin's lifelong mining and sifting in his journals of an authentic language in pursuit of poetry in Irish is one of the most remarkable literary stories of Ireland in the twentieth century. Norman MacCaig's comment about his fellow Scottish poet, Sorley MacGill-Eain writing in Gaelic, firmly applies here: 'Nobody does that except for the deepest and most compulsive reasons.'

Those 'reasons' might well be a matter of interesting speculation, and revealing insight, especially around the whole area of mother tongue and father language, and what we now have come to understand by compulsion. Ó Ríordáin's poetry issues from his exploration of the unnavigated and terrifying depths of the unconscious. All authentic lives are subject to terror, as is clear from his diaries. It is the interpenetration of both languages, synergized in his work as two functioning lungs, which made all the difference.

Innti, the poetry journal first published in 1970 as a broadsheet, owes its title to an adverbial phrase from the speech of an individual in West Kerry. Through *Innti*, the *caint na ndaoine* slogan of early Revivalist writers was turned on its head to become *daoine ag caint*. Poems for the *Innti* generation would be grounded in living speech, following more 'Pound's' – as in Ó

Ríordáin's poem 'An Feairín' ('The Maneen') – than Ezra Pound's advice. Both Máirtín Ó Direáin, that great dignified man, and Seán Ó Ríordáin, had poems in the first edition. Michael Davitt (1950-2005), the poet and founding editor of *Innti* with fellow-poet Gabriel Rosenstock and the musician Con Ó Drisceoil, was the main catalyst of change. He had been at school in the North Monastery, where Seán Ó Ríordáin too had attended. Charismatic, a showman and shaman, he had one foot planted firmly in West Kerry and the other, exploratory, on the campus of University College Cork.

Like many campus initiatives of its time, *Innti* turned the course of poetry in Irish toward the demotic and formal experimentation. It admitted a frank sexuality, and presented a brazen, youthful face to the world. In time, the Irish language lyric poem would break open on its pages. The initial campus energy was sustained through around 12 editions, and the most important contemporary poets would be associated with it. Michael Davitt's editorial hand was always firmly on the tiller, but he engaged editorially with others besides Gabriel Rosenstock – Louis de Paor, Proinsias Ní Dhorchaí especially – to bring the journal forward as the national journal of poetry in Irish. It displaced the monthly literary magazine *Comhar*, as the main publishing conduit for new poetry, but not before *Comhar* itself had nurtured some of the emerging poets under the editorship of Eoghan Ó hAnluain and threw open its pages later with Proinsias Ní Dhorchaí as editor.

Michael Davitt's own poetry is marked throughout his work by a cinematic eye, filtered through a varying but intense focus, as if the *manner* of recording reality were the act of revealing the poetic insight itself. In a style of hyper-realism at times, it has all the elements of the wideshot panorama to the close-up, phrased in an uncompromising, contemporaneous language of the now, humorous, sometimes searing, always adjectivally unfrocked and with a tensile beauty in lines of his own tuning. That tuning is as much a matter of his own inner ear as his unerring instinct for calibrating newly-minted words and terms with the resonance of living speech. His conscious project of emulating Bob Dylan has yet to be examined in any meaningful way – his first collection *Gleann ar Ghleann* (1982) marks *Blonde on Blonde,* but his second collection, *Bligeard Sráide* (1983), which has the look at least of *Self-Portrait,* has an iconic status in contemporary Irish poetry. There is a metallic, lyrical tension at the core of his work, in the tone beneath his overlying style, which is mysterious – 'Meirg agus Lios Luachra' – and which is possibly never definitively resolved but from which there is a joyful, sensual and easeful respite in the later collections – *Fardoras* (2003) – and especially in the suite of poems which gives its title to his last collection, *Seiming Soir* (2004).

Innti was at its core, a *non*-academic initiative. While there are no absolute breaks with the past, *Innti* was in many respects *sui generis*. Gabriel

Rosenstock's wide reading of literature, his editorial involvement with *Motus*, the English language literary magazine, and his mediation of the world of English poetry through *Innti* had a major influence on *Innti's* initial development. But *Innti* owed more to Gaeltacht-speak, rock 'n roll and the Sixties' folk revival, the cinema and whatever – you're – having – yourself, than to any early reading of William Carlos Williams, Frank O'Hara or Robert Frost if not Eliot or E.E. Cummings and French poetry. *Sean-nós* too, an art form in itself at its best and brought alive by Seán Ó Riada both on disc and in his invitations to singers to perform on campus, was a further important point of entry into the language.

The Seáin Triumvirate in University College Cork – Ó Riada, Ó Ríordáin and Ó Tuama – created an atmosphere in which exuberance, at least, could thrive. Seán Ó Tuama's *An Grá in Amhráin na nDaoine* and *Caoineadh Airt Uí Laoghaire* (1961) seemed to have a synchronicity with the age. But in many respects it was Ó Riada, like Hamlet's ghost, who had the most profound influence – as if he were playing not only the language of music, but the music of a language on a national and world stage. It was Ó Riada who had clasped the classical heritage of poetry and song of a language-community, and it was he who forged his own vital linkage with a community which allows artistic work to truly come alive and thrive. It is through Ó Riada that poets, in English and in Irish, can legitimately claim that heritage as their own. It was highly ironic that Seán Ó Riada, who travelled the world, had made his home in Cúil Aodha, while the Sixties' generation of learners of Irish and their teachers from Cork city headed west past his door to Kerry.

Nuala Ní Dhomhnaill and the Donegal poet Cathal Ó Searcaigh, who is as much an *Innti* poet in spirit as any, have stayed close to their own language communities. Nuala Ní Dhomhnaill's voice is as much her own as ancestral, surging through the marvellous psychic drama of her poems especially in *An Dealg Droighin* (1981) and *Feis* (1991). Her outpourings on the page are seemingly unmediated by formal rigours as we knew them, before Nuala, or might have wished them, but are turbo-driven by a more immediate urgency. It is as if an ancestral community were not so much thinking through her as feeling through her, in the poem's present tense, with the authentic voices of *mná ag caint*. She, indeed, is the inheritor of *banseanchas* with the great heave of her poems washing up on the bare page. She achieved an untrammelled, almost industrial access to the unconscious through her hard work on folklore and storytelling and through her wide reading. She has great humour and handles the big themes as assuredly as the everyday, household traumas of suburbia which can also of course become big themes. She refeminised the territory, and swept away much of the aridity of the Revivalist spirit. The whiplash of some of her lines is her own making as much as the pickled variety of Corca Dhuibhne speech. It is understandable that many contemporary poets in English would have wanted to translate her work, Michael Hartnett early on and Paul Muldoon later in *The Astrakhan Cloak* (1992). However, the handing over of the original work has major consequences, one of them being John McInnes's quip, as quoted in *An Tuil* (1999), the anthology of 20th Century Scottish Gaelic Poetry, by the editor Ronald Black: 'It loses something in the original'.

It is perhaps, a matter of how we believe a poem might live a life. Either in terms of its own integrity, hoping that it might make room for itself, or with the help of others. There is not much, now, to support the belief that an Irish language poem might live a life through that natural flowing into a common stream. It is not entirely injudicious to think that it might be through translation into English that the original might bounce back in unexpected ways. However, translation into English of contemporary Irish language poetry can selectively reduce the poem itself and undermine the possibilities of forms of further evolving life for the original poem. A recent commentator suggested, while reviewing a collection in Irish, that the originals might have been written in English and subsequently translated into Irish. This might well be true, but is a masquerade, a subterfuge too far for any intelligent engagement with real poems in Irish.

Gabriel Rosenstock is the great innovator of his generation, and his first collection *Suzanne sa Seomra Folctha* (1973) still has great charm – it already marks out the course that Gabriel's path through poetry would take, original work and translations forming part of the whole. It bridged the generations and brought the Irish language poem into domains it had never known. His 'Laoi an Rua-Indiaigh Dhíbeartha' stands totemically on its own. 'Deireadh Seachtaine na Martinis Dry' still has that wonderful tone of world-weariness and urbanity of an underrated *film noir*. His prodigious if not bewildering output can at times mask his achievements. He has translated from many languages into Irish and has developed the *haiku*. His poetry and books for children are often a collaboration with visual artists, and he more than anyone has actively sought to engage others in the world of the poem in Irish. He has a mordant wit and a scarifying lyricism. Inclined to the Gothic, his greatest gift to the Irish language poem is his stance as outsider. He has turned the poem in Irish inside out, and outside in – *Conlán*, a selection of Heaney poems – and has often left his contemporaries scorched in his slipstream. In many respects, Rosenstock's achievements have exposed the threadbare texture of the range of writing in the Irish language. At times our hope for him would be that he would have more stamina in pursuing the possibilities of individual poems. It could well be that, in time, the language itself might catch up with him. It is more likely that, in some future domain, his work will be seen as how poems in Irish might have been.

The form of what constitutes a poem, whatever its mode, is of fundamental importance to the essential life of the poem. A poem must be able to hold its own ground. It is very difficult to see, now, how any poem in Irish might hold its ground. In Irish, because of a residual collective neurosis serving the cause of the language and active individual neuroses serving the cause of poetry, together with little or no critical judgement and uninspired academic performance, the health of the poem itself is indeed precarious. The first responsibility of the poet is to serve the poem itself. The matter of translation downwards, as in Seamus Deane's phrase in reference to Joyce, and translation *inwards* into the internal dynamics of the poem itself, is a process that can take a lifetime but it is what serves the poem. In an age which serves the poet more than the poem it is difficult to sustain the work which, in its own time, results in real poems.

Cathal Ó Searcaigh's joyous celebration of his own people and place in North West Donegal, his buoyant homo-eroticism, is both convincing and infectious. He has a geographic range from Mucais to Nepal. Reading the bulk of his poems in the original *Ag Tnúth Leis an tSolas* (2000), something happens. A boyishness comes alive in his imaginative landscape, marvelling at the humanity of it all, which affirms a boyishness in ourselves. This can be easily and unjustifiably misconstrued. If there is harshness there – 'Gort na gCnámh' – it is in the suffering inflicted by human beings through an inability to love and receive love. His portraits of older people are superb, and awaken us to our own intimacy by our participation as listeners to, and readers of his own relationships. One of the consistent aspects of his work is his musical phrasing, broken in unexpected places to arrest the ear. His emotional range gathers us in with its unadulterated exuberance, especially in his love poems. His earlier work struggled with the displacement to the city from his native Donegal Gaeltacht, in pursuit of his beloved beats. While he resolved the matter in his grounding of the work in his own place, it has also kept the development of a broader emotional range in check. It is not merely an issue of sentimentality, but more of growing away from the fold, from being, literally, penned in.

The relationship between the poem in Irish and music has never been properly explored, due in no small measure to the scholarly obsession with the fractured text of the language and semantics. Language carries meaningfulness beyond semantics, perhaps into some area of the collective unconscious. The Gaelic poets of Scotland understood this far more clearly than their brothers and sisters in Ireland. In Ireland, we have nothing to rival 'Moladh Beinn Dobhrainn, Birlinn Chlann Raghnaill' or Somhairle Mac Gill-Eain.

The sounds of Irish poetry move us in mysterious ways. The language itself has a strange hold on us, beyond reasonableness. It is possible to view the vast panoply of Irish poetry, for example, as a language with an unwritten musical notation, the music of itself. One of the tasks in dealing with it is to absorb it aurally as much as to read it. The result of this is a translation into itself. In that way, the Irish language can become a 'foreign language' of unimagined richness.

On a simpler level, if we listen to two songs by Elizabeth Cronin, 'Uncle Rat' from the English tradition and the milking chant 'Raghadsa ó thuaidh leat a bhó', we may experience almost two universes, one in the parlour and the other in the cowshed. They probably met in the kitchen. On another level, of equal simplicity, we could read aloud the wonderful, witty, *Agallamh na Seanórach*, the colloquy of Oisín and Pádraig, and experience the text in its full instrumental range with all its clashing symbols. Old Irish could well be heard as heavy metal, the Court Poetry as baroque, the Love Songs as R&B with its development into *sean-nós* as blues, and contemporary poetry since the early 1970s as rock 'n roll and jazz! It may be only through an exploration of its own music, now, that the poem in Irish might have a real life of its own. This seems to have been firmly grasped by Louis de Paor and the Belfast poet Gearóid MacLochlainn.

One of the primary characteristics of poetry and song in the Irish language, as long as it has been produced on and off the island of Ireland has been a love of small things. It is as if the Irish always knew that it could never be otherwise, and then got on with fully inhabiting their imaginative world. Whether composed by named authors or anonymously, it has issued from a collective, intimate consciousness, earthed in the ground of collective values but often with an unearthly reach. Its unfailing appeal has always been to affirm humanity, the human dimension of our being in this world and more often than not of our being in an otherworld. The mainstay of the poem in Irish may not be to wear the world's cloak through whatever means, but to wear its own cloak as a loose garment. This is not an appeal for 'nativism' or even atavism, merely a statement of belief in the intrinsic value of the poem itself.

Louis de Paor has reversed the usual relationship of the text in Irish with its translated version – *Ag Greadadh Bas sa Reilig/Clapping in the Cemetery* (2005) – by placing his original poem on the facing right page, and his collaborative English versions on the left. This is an important statement of intent. Interestingly, for an Irish langauge reader the translations offer extended glosses on the originals. A 'second-wave' member of the *Innti* generation, together with Colm Breathnach, he has a painterly eye and an acute intelligence. His sensual imagery is easy on the eye – 'Aonach na dTorthaí' - and his poems are remarkable for their shadings and colours. His inversions, or new connections – 'Fabhalscéal' – release a whole new way of *seeing* through the Irish language. He, too, has undertaken his own filtration of home, spending time in Australia, and has further extended the range of the city in Irish language poetry. His brilliance is, literally, dazzling. If that leads at times to what can seem like rhetoric or overstatement, it may be because the poem powers ahead, leaving the original impetus stranded. But invariably, he manages to retrieve it – 'Corcach' – as if he knew best himself that he needed to take the long way around, home.

Colm Breathnach is the most grounded of the contemporary poets in the classical South Munster mould. The beat and measure of his lines dance off the floor to tunes we think we know. While his imagination travels by shadow and often through undergrowth, there is an enduring solidity at the core of his work which is the true mark of a master craftsman. He is honest and direct, never an actor in his own poems. His tone is restrained, never pushing the decibel level beyond the limiter, and he delivers his work with what can seem like forensic detachment at times. A form of understatement, it is also the mark of true feeling. His collection *Scáthach* (1994) still reads like one seamless poem in many voices, both male and female. His organisation of the collection would seem to wish it to be so. 'Fáschoill' is a poem of great integrity to return to, again and again. He, too, has journeyed towards that sublimation of the male and female form, mother and father, into the one form. His *An Fear Marbh* (1998) is a heartbreaking collection for his dead father, full of regret, but a relationship resolved. Some of those poems, at least, *have* gone into the common stream. For a poet of great integrity who has stayed close-hauled to the original call, it is time for himself, perhaps, to allow versions in English translation to take him on a broader reach.

Much the same applies to Biddy Jenkinson, who draws together in her *Fantasia Entymologiae et Zoologiae*, as it were, that offshoot stream of *Innti* and what could be called the textual literary tradition of Leinster and other territories. She too has resisted the pull of translation. Her poems can go off like fireworks, or ground us – 'Eanáir 1991'; '15 Eanáir 1991' – in the locally globalised inhumanity of the now. Biddy Jenkinson, for all her seemingly impromptu references to sexual organs, is a deeply *moral* poet, as for example, was Eoghan Ó Tuairisc. In many respects, she is working out of that important literary branch of writing in Irish – represented by Ó Tuairisc, Rita Kelly, Conleth Ellis, Mícheál Ó hUanacháin and others – which can be as difficult to reach as to fix in place. She is playful and has an exhuberant lightness of touch, with that specific humour of the poem as almost a found object. The Biddy Jenkinson *character* is as interesting in the poems as her flights of fancy and her close-up observations of the natural world. If the thinness of her lines is sometimes problematic, she mostly manages to bring off the poem with great panache and that leavening of the spirit which is the hallmark of her work.

Many others' poems need to be looked at, and addressed, especially Gearóid MacLochlainn's work. If there is a vibrant, new contemporary voice in Irish language poetry, Gearóid's is it. Aifric MacAodha's first collection is also due, and much expected. Tomás Mac Síomóin was a very important presence during the early years of *Innti*, and his *Damhna agus Dánta Eile(1974)* especially, marked a strong new voice in Irish poetry. He also worked the longer and narrative poem, but in latter years has given his attention to prose. However, pressure of space will not allow such a review for now.

Much has been achieved in the poetry of the past forty years in Irish. It has seen much individual achievement, international performance and recognition. While the main focus in that period has been on the poets of Northern Ireland, a coherent and highly significant body of work continued to evolve in Irish, giving voice to another very contemporary Irelandness. It would be interesting, too, to explore the range and nature of that voice through the poets who work out of that same Munster tradition in the English language - Paddy Galvin, Greg Delanty, Theo Dorgan, Gerry Murphy, Bob Welch, Tom McCarthy, Maurice Riordan, Bernard O'Donoghue, Gregory O'Donoghue and Seán Dunne.

An Irish language poet may perform to an audience of five thousand in Buenos Aires and fifteen – on a lucky night – in Ballyhaunis, more if the work were in Polish or Portuguese. Poetry itself has become marginalised, its status diminished on the outer edge of our field of vision. Much of our hopes for what the poem in Irish might achieve, in its further evolutionary forms, are groundless. The ground itself has shifted and even opened up under the poem. The poem in Irish is in freefall. Literacy in the language has all but collapsed in that same period since 1968.

Broadcasting and newspaper journalism are now working the oral and written text of the language to the degree that a public just about tolerates and enjoys, and the broadcasters are the contemporary storytellers and *seanchaithe*. In many respects, this is quite healthy. But there is little room for the real poem, that form of emotional and intellectual engagement with the world that can change our lives. A new home must be found for the poem in Irish. Translation outwards, is of course, a reality of our lives. But the poem in Irish now must be constructed out of thin air. Some of the best of the lyric poems in Old Irish, too, were also plucked out of the air. As the possibilities of a poetry in contemporary Irish have diminished completely, a new interest emerges in the soundscapes of the classical language, of unchanging forms. This is a sort of evolution backwards. The ancient vernacular has extraordinary endurance.

Even if the poem in Irish has become an anchronism, the original call still rings true. The Blasket Island writer Tomás Ó Criomhthain in *Allagar na hInise,* a true offshore man and probably aware of the initial paradox in reverse, says on one of the days of his life:

> *Tar éis dinnéir dom, buailim siar chun an ghoirt úd go mbraithim pé díth sláinte a bhí orm ag dul ann dom, ag scaradh liom le linn é fhágaint dom, buíochas mór le Dia.* (After dinner I head back to that piece of ground where I feel any ill-health that I had going there lifting from me as I leave there, great thanks be to God.)

The ground of the poem has always been the key.

If what heeding the call can seem, in hindsight, 'a need for legitimate foolishness' in a phrase of the psychoanlyst Otto Rank, what sustains it is the ongoing revelation in poems of the truths of our lives. Why would we then, in further foolishness, not proceed further out of the original daze? The Anglican theologian, H. A. Williams, refers in his work *The Joy of God* to something very close to what happens in the world of the poem: 'The joy of God lies waiting with infinite patience for the appointed time, working continuously with every kind of recaltricant raw material, until it delivers as golden what formerly was brazen.'

The original promise of the poem still rings true.

John Griffin

The Knife of Conscience: The Enduring Value of Patrick Kavanagh's Poetry

Although Patrick Kavanagh is one of Ireland's most popular and beloved poets, studied by generations of Irish school children, and considered along with Yeats the most important poet of the last century, his work is still relatively neglected abroad. He has not yet taken his rightful place on the larger literary stage[1]. Why is this? Is his appeal regional and insular only, or does it have a wider international allure? Kavanagh himself believed that all themes as events of epic import began locally, even the *Iliad* he claimed was made from a local row, but to have that far-reaching, universal point of view, a poet must 'possess the right kind of sensitive courage and the right kind of sensitive humility'. Kavanagh's emblems and touchstones were mostly rural and domestic but their outlook was exclusively cosmopolitan, and his famous distinction between the parochial and provincial mentalities was drawn precisely to defend this view. The poet had a cranky and domineering personality and became notorious in Dublin for his brash critical pronouncements, but this should not tempt us into complacency or to confusing the legacy of that personality with the superlative merit of his poetry.

Kavanagh occupies a pivotal place in the Irish canon. This much is certain. He arrived at a time of great transition when the newly independent nation was seeking to define its own unique identity. In many ways he provided an antidote to the sentimental idealizations of the Celtic Literary Revival: here was the genuine article these post-romantics had only apprehended at a distance and as a disembodied, mythic ideal. What's more, this living specimen not only spoke and sang, he also ranted and raved and even seemed quite

---

[1] Antoinette Quinn has rendered an incomparable service to Kavanagh studies and her two landmark books, the biography and critical study, as well as her numerous editions of his works, have paid a long overdue debt of scholarship to the poet's legacy. Thanks to Quinn's ground-breaking work, the Kavanagh oeuvre may finally have what it has hitherto lacked, a solid foundation for serious scholarship. A similar service was paid in America by the poet's brother Peter who first published his letters and uncollected prose and made available a more comprehensive edition of the poems. Peter also printed an unfinished novel as well as a most valuable bibliography. But it's not as though Kavanagh hadn't received other critical attention; he had; there were monographs by Alan Warner, John Nemo and Darcy O'Brien, et al., and more recently Sr. Una Agnew and Tom Stack have extended the scope of Kavanagh studies. Also, the number of Irish writers and poets who have written about him and acknowledged some debt to his work is quite staggering.

mad. At first, he wrote what he thought was expected of him, the authentic 'peasant quality', and he achieved a measure of success with it, but he soon came to repudiate and attack this as a betrayal of poetic truth[2]. The next phase of his work set him against the literary establishment and if Kavanagh's place is secured by anything today, it is the important contribution he made to the tradition by challenging it.

The Great Hunger is his most sustained assault on the assumptions of the Celtic Revival and the spiritual underpinnings of De Valera's new republic. Here Yeats' Connemara fisherman meets Kavanagh's Patrick Maguire. The two square off and it's quickly apparent which creation is the more authentic. Kavanagh realized the crucial ground he had broken and staked out with Maguire and this perspective framed the rest of his writing career. He assumed the mantle of authentic spokesman for the peasant and opposed it to anything that smacked of imposture or masquerade. He would not tolerate mummery, exploitation, expropriation or misrepresentation. His crusade was to rout all humbug and pretension. In article after article, essay after essay, poem after poem he attacked the shibboleths of the new republic and whatever he considered artificial, mediocre or inauthentic. He was contrarian, uncompromising, vituperative and acerbic. He waylaid his opponents with lethal efficiency and delivered sweeping pronouncements on their lifetime's work[3]. Standards must be defended, he argued, and he was just the man to do it. He defined virtue as 'the ability to tell the truth even when it doesn't serve your own self-interest'. His friends and foes alike felt the lash of his tongue.

But then the pendulum swung the other way and Kavanagh found himself reaping his own whirlwind. A libel suit he filed backfired and his enemies retaliated. All the forces he had offended were now concentrated in one man, the former Prime Minister and barrister John A. Costello, who turned the tables in the courtroom and put the plaintiff on the defence[4]. Kavanagh was vanquished and very publicly humiliated. He was also penniless and

---

[2] Kavanagh published his first lyrics in George Russell's [AE's] *Irish Statesman*. These poems are pure sentimental whimsy and meet all the criteria of the 'Peasant Quality'. It was on their basis and the success of *Ploughman and Other Poems* (1936) that Kavanagh wrote the novel, *The Green Fool*. He later came to repudiate these early works.

[3] Consider for example his damning review of Maurice Walsh's novel, *The Hill is Mine*, in *The Irish Times* in 1940, which launched the career of Myles Na gCopaleen. His essay 'The Gallivanting Poet' was a devastating blow to the life work of F.R. Higgins, and his attack on Frank O'Connor in 'Coloured Balloons: A Study of Frank O'Connor' wounded O'Connor deeply.

[4] Peter always claimed that Costello used the same strategy in the trial as Sir Edward Carson had used against Oscar Wilde: Patrick was cross-examined for 13 hours and the trial took on a circus atmosphere in Dublin.

ill. Diagnosed with lung cancer immediately after the trial, he had to be hospitalized and have a lung removed. This defeat hit him hard. If he chose to see in it a touch of the Grand Inquisitor, the wind was also fairly knocked out of him. So he returned to source. He recuperated by rediscovering the very truths that had launched his literary career. His epiphany was to end where he began, and he now wrote simple but passionate lyrics about nature and ordinary things: 'There are two kinds of simplicity,' he said, 'the simplicity of going away and the simplicity of return. The last is the ultimate in sophistication.' He rediscovered his love of the sonnet form too ('the vehicle for the expression of love') and used it to exquisite effect in the stunning 'Canal Poems'. This final flowering in the years 1956-59 was Kavanagh's last hurrah. He composed then many of his poems on which his reputation justifiably stands. He had come full circle and realized that the profoundest truths lay in 'common and banal' things, 'the casual, insignificant little things you would be ashamed to talk of publicly.' He asserted:

> Naming these things is the love-act and its pledge;
> For we must record love's mystery without claptrap,
> Snatch out of time the passionate transitory[5].

II

Kavanagh's poetic opportunity coincided with the realization that there was a huge gap between the sentimentalised version of the rustic life he had lived and that life in reality: he knew first-hand how brutal and emasculating the medieval peasant life really was. There was little charm in it, no bucolic allure in poverty and ignorance and certainly no romance in hardship or repression. If Ireland was seeking to define itself in ideal terms by romanticizing all the adversity he had endured, then he would give voice to the truth. He would disabuse the literary establishment of all its jingoistic myths and lies and present the harsh reality. After all, he was the authority[6]. His poetic voice sprang from this impulse and grew to give expression to contempt for all kinds of counterfeit sentiment. Anything he thought was fake or dishonest met with

---

[5] 'The Hospital'.

[6] 'It took me many years to work myself free from that formula for literature which laid all the stress on whether it was Irish or not. For twenty years I wrote according to the dispensation of this Irish school. The appraisers of the school all agreed that I had my roots in the soil, was one of the people and that I was an authentic voice. What the alleged poetry lover loved was the Irishness of a thing. Irishness is a form of anti-art. A way of posing as a poet without actually being one.' *Self-Portrait*.

his unmitigated opprobrium. He opposed his simple Antaeus-like lyricism to what he considered the laboured and ossified verses of the Revivalists[7]. If there is one virtue in Kavanagh's poetry (and criticism) it is that it is consistently and brutally honest. He believed that true patronage consisted as much in keeping the wrong sort down as in assisting the right kind up. This takes daring and confidence as well as disinterestedness towards one's own prospects, which Kavanagh had, but above all he was a sincere poet.

This is why he was so dismissive of his own work: he generally emphasised its flaws, which is meritorious surely, but only if backed by the rarer goods. Kavanagh had those rarer goods and composed some of the most sublime lyrics, but he was also inconsistent, lazy, flippant, and rather inclined to put expediency over self-discipline and veracity before rigour. He squandered his gifts and his output was uneven to say the least[8]. Some of the poems do not rise above the level of doggerel, others surrender to pat emotion and rancour, and quite a number of them could have used the discriminating eye of a good editor. But the finer poems at the core of his output deserve our scrutiny and respect and these are the poems that will endure[9].

In the poems that count, Kavanagh had cultivated a voice that was transcendent, prophetic, incorruptible and supremely authoritarian. The lesser poems are often characterized by a stridency and bitterness not compensated for by their honesty or sincerity. When he forgot his dignity, his art suffered and his tone became shrill and caustic, even vengeful. It is sometimes a very fine line that separates the two, especially when those qualities he used to articulate his aesthetic creed were the same ones that forced him into internal exile and orphaned his imagination. He expresses this beautifully in the poem 'Innocence':

---

[7] 'Seán O'Faoláin suggested, and several other superficial critics supported him, that I was only interested in flat reality; that I had dung in my mouth, that I only understood the small farm. For everything outside that I had no understanding or love. Nothing could be farther from the truth. What I seek and love when I find is the whiskey of the imagination, not the bread and butter of "reality." This is the thing I seek in writing and this is the thing I most dreadfully miss in the verse that is being written in this country these days. The poems being written are like perfectly laid-out [37] corpses on a slab. They are perfectly shaped and perfectly dead. There is nothing you can say to the dead or about the dead. Life is everything. Life is what we love. The spark of life justifies the most indifferent body, makes it beautiful.' *The Bell* 16, 1 (April 1948), pp.36-43.

[8] Speaking of output, Kavanagh once remarked, *What's **Output**? What about Gerard Manley Hopkins? Would you judge him by — output? Two or three books will say all a writer has to say.*

[9] I have in mind such poems as 'Inniskeen Road: July Evening', 'Shancoduff', 'Memory of My Father', 'A Christmas Childhood', 'Spraying the Potatoes', 'Why Sorrow', 'The Great Hunger', 'Lough Derg', 'Advent', 'Peace', 'Father Mat', 'In Memory of My Mother', 'Ragland Road', 'Jungle', 'Ant-Natal Dream', 'Kerr's Ass', 'Innocence', 'Epic', 'God in Woman', 'Having Confessed' and most of the poems that Antoinette Quinn has collected in the years 1956-59.

> They laughed at one I loved –
> The triangular hill that hung
> Under the Big Forth. They said
> That I was bounded by the whitethorn hedges
> Of the little farm and did not know the world.
> But I knew that love's doorway to life
> Is the same doorway everywhere.

This was Kavanagh's keenest poetic insight, and the source of his original vision, the notion that the expansiveness of the whole world inhered in the same 'stony grey soil' that 'burgled his bank of youth' and 'clogged his feet [that] had the poise and stride of Apollo'. He said that 'to get to know even a small field was a lifetime's exploration'[10] and he vacillated for the rest of his life between love and disdain for this 'mandrel strained ... coulter blunted' earth, yet his mind and heart always returned to it. It was his poetic Omphalos[11].

Kavanagh's poetry enacts a peculiar kind of alienation. To quote Seamus Heaney, he became an 'inner émigré'[12], an exile in his own homeland, for as soon as he rejected that first fog of unknowing, the black earth of Monaghan, he spent the rest of his days struggling to get back to it. He realized too late 'there is no going back' and that 'the happiness of that time consisted in its unconsciousness. When we are unconscious,' he said, 'we are close to the eternal: we have to shut our eyes to see our way to heaven'[13]. Poetry made him an outcast and put a kink in him, and the price he paid was loneliness and poverty.

Peter once remarked to me that he pursued an academic career so that Patrick wouldn't have to. He wanted to keep him safe in the 'right kind of ignorance', by which he meant free of scholarship. This theme runs throughout the poetry where we even find open hostility to erudition. We are used to poets today being highly educated and authoring if not quite scholarly essays then certainly polished, methodic and learned ones. Many of the best poets are not only public intellectuals, they also teach at universities.

---

[10] Recording, *Almost Everything*.

[11] 'I would say that, as a poet, I was born in or about nineteen-fifty-five, the place of my birth being the banks of the Grand Canal. Thirty years earlier Shancoduff's watery hills could have done the trick, but I was too thick to take the hint. Curious this, how I had started out with the right simplicity, indifferent to crude reason and then ploughed my way through complexities and anger, hatred and ill-will towards the faults of man, and came back to where I started.' *Self-Portrait*.

[12] Seamus Heaney, 'Exposure', *North*.

[13] Recording, *Almost Everything*.

Kavanagh wasn't widely-read at all, his formal education concluded at the age of 13 and he never wrote what could be considered a scholarly essay. He was an autodidact and believed that we get to our destiny in the end – 'if the potentialities are there,' he wrote, 'it is almost certain that they will find a way out; they will burst a road'.

> Now I have to sit down and think
> a world into existence; you cannot borrow
> anyone else's ...

Kavanagh placed great store in ignorance, albeit his own brand of ignorance, which accepts the limits of knowledge in the face of mystery or the unknown, in other words, a sort of learned ignorance or belief that 'the face of truth is often most truly reflected in the mirror of folly'.

Whatever explains the comparative dearth of scholarly material on Kavanagh's work might also suggest why he is still not widely known abroad: the poetry is not dissertation-friendly and doesn't offer anything in the way of consistency or systematic unity – to a large extent it remains undefinable and almost certainly unclassifiable. It is full of revisions, reversals, contradictions, antithetical pronouncements and unpredictable twists and turns. In one poem Kavanagh might endorse Catholic orthodoxy and then in the very next completely reject that view, or he may love the thing he later excoriates, and each expression seems somehow true to his vision. One could explicate individual poems and say why they are crucial but this would be no guide for what might follow. The poetry demands to be taken on its own terms because it is its own frame of reference, its own measure and end, totally self-contained and non-derivative[14]. Kavanagh articulated an aesthetic manifesto[15], but it must be culled from his opus, and what emerges is something truly original, rife with humour, poetically independent, philosophically authentic and always riveting. He was a diamond in the rough but a diamond withal, and buried in the depths of shale his crystal still shines with a pure and intense white light. He was a mystic and a visionary, a guiding star, and his work will endure.

---

[14] Kavanagh put it this way, *I am, as Napoleon said, my own ancestors*.

[15] He considered poetry a holy, enchanted and mystical enterprise and saw the poet as one imbued with vatic qualities whose sacred office is to disseminate immutable truths and absolute standards.

Eleanor Hooker

John Hewitt: Ulster Poet

Poet and Socialist John Hewitt (1907-1987) is remembered and celebrated in his birthplace of Northern Ireland. The John Hewitt Society, established in 1987, the year of Hewitt's death, commemorates the life and work of Hewitt with cultural events throughout the year. Its annual one-day Spring Festival and *John Hewitt International Summer School* is well renowned. The Society's mission is 'to encourage debate, understanding, tolerance and acceptance of cultural diversity' in keeping with Hewitt's own philosophy. A second, and rather unusual, establishment that celebrates Hewitt and his work is the John Hewitt Bar. The bar was founded to generate income for its owners, The Belfast Unemployed Resource Centre, and was officially opened by John Hewitt, Freeman of Belfast, in 1983.

John Hewitt is less well known outside Northern Ireland than other poets of his calibre, but the reason for this is unclear. Could it be that without a more insistent advocate, his poetry is no longer being read and thus forgotten? Perhaps the poetic themes that emerged from more recent political upheavals in Northern Ireland have overshadowed and displaced Hewitt's in the public's imagination.

To appreciate the poetry of John Hewitt, one has to understand and to accept the extent to which his origins and his lineage within the cultural and political landscape of Northern Ireland profoundly informs his work. Much of his poetry resolutely describes *Ulsterness* in all its permutations. It may be this fact that arouses such varying responses to his poetry when it is read or critically examined today. In his essay 'John Hewitt and memory: a reflection' *(The Literature of Ireland; Culture and Criticism),* Terence Brown describes Hewitt as a poet of 'memory and loss'. Gerald Dawe, in 'Against Piety: John Hewitt' *(The Proper WORD; Collected Criticism, Ireland, Poetry, Politics)*, suggests that Hewitt's poetry explores 'roots' and 'horizons'. Derek Mahon, in his book *Journalism*, writes that Hewitt *'was* a regional poet... an *Ulster* poet, by his own definition', and Fred Johnston, in his review of Hewitt's *Collected Poems*, writes that 'Hewitt was concerned with the greater, more quilted view of Ulsterness and, by implication, a greater good'. The question of origin in any context is often fraught, particularly in Northern Ireland where it is weighted with the additional burden of tribal allegiance and obligation.

John Hewitt was born in Belfast into a Methodist family. He was educated at Agnes Street National School, where his father was headmaster, and Methodist College secondary school. He went on to read English at Queen's

University, Belfast. In his early twenties Hewitt began to reject the teachings of his Methodist upbringing in favour of a more secular life, but not without uncertainty. His poetry reflects that wavering non-conformist conscience.

Hewitt's desire to own legitimacy of place and heritage as a Protestant Irish Ulsterman alongside his fellow Irishmen is inscribed in the imagined landscape of many of his poems. Hewitt promoted Ulster Regionalism as a cultural solution to the region's difficulties. He believed that allegiance to one's roots and language could be a point of unity and not division. In keeping with the deep political division of the time, his ideas were not popular with either the Unionists, who thought him pro-Republican, or the Republicans, who thought him Pro-Unionist. It was felt that this contributed to Hewitt's failure in his bid for a promotion to Director at the Belfast Museum and Art Gallery, and in 1953 he moved to Coventry. There he worked as Director of the Herbert Art Gallery and Museum until his retirement in 1972. By all accounts this episode in Hewitt's life caused him considerable distress.

Following his retirement, Hewitt returned to Northern Ireland. By this time it was a very troubled province. Hewitt wrote prolifically and his interest in the notion of cultural regionalism took expression in the publication of his anthology *Rhyming Weavers and Other Country Poets of Antrim and Down* (1974). This book celebrates the lives and work of nineteenth century Protestant radicals who wrote dialect verse in Ulster-Scots vernacular. Coincidentally, at the same time Seamus Heaney was also using the vernacular to establish his distinctive Ulster identity.

In his poetry Hewitt worries about his Ulster Protestant Planter identity, yet much of his work positively asserts his right to that identity. He insists that the Ulster writer 'must be a *rooted* man. He must carry the native tang of his idiom like the native dust on his sleeve; otherwise he is an airy internationalist, thistledown, a twig in a stream'.

In his poem 'An Ulsterman', he writes,

> This is my country. If my people came
> From England here four centuries ago,
> The only trace that's left is my name.

In this poem Hewitt makes no apology for his fidelity to his inheritance; 'I will cling to the inflexions of my origin'. He goes on to ask whether it is not legitimate that he should 'remonstrate' when 'creed-crazed zealots and the ignorant crowd' have made the streets of Northern Ireland 'a byword of offence', concluding that 'My heritage is not their violence'. Hewitt is not afraid to confront and express his intolerance of sectarian violence on both sides of the 'divide'.

Many of Hewitt's poems give a sense of thinking aloud, of working through a conundrum towards a not entirely satisfactory conclusion, either for the poet or his reader. In 'Conacre' (1943), Hewitt's mood moves from diffidence and a discrete self-awareness of his attachment, to the loveliness of the landscape earlier in the poem, and then to a declaration and a longing.

> This is my home and country. Later on
> Perhaps I'll find this nation is my own;
> But here and now it is enough to love
> This faulted ledge.

Further on in the same poem and with an abrupt, almost venomous change in mood, Hewitt describes the nature, as he sees it, of the rural inhabitants of Northern Ireland. He describes a ghoulish, greedy people, for whom religion is also their commerce. Yet having made his criticism, Hewitt admonishes himself for being 'too savage'. He remembers the kindness and hospitality of those same rural people and concludes that he must leave off from his 'wilful attitude'. As a city dweller Hewitt longs for assimilation into the countryside, but he is painfully attentive to the fact that he remains outside and outsider.

> I know my farmer and my farmer's wife,
> the squalid focus of their huxter life,
> the grime-veined fists, the thick rheumatic legs,
> the cracked voice gloating on the price of eggs,
> the miser's Bible and the tedious aim
> to add another boggy acre to the name.

And yet this is too savage.

This quote from 'Conacre' has echoes of Yeats' poem 'September 1913', which describes the nature of the merchant class city dweller as opposed to the farmer. Interestingly, both poets characterise their respective groups in the same hostile terms; as ignorant and greedy and for whom religion is only another commodity. However, there is a crucial difference. Whereas Yeats' accusations run the length of his poem, offering no redeeming features in his subject, Hewitt becomes self-reflective, stops himself, and will not make all rural dwellers a type.

> What need you, being come to sense,
> But fumble in a greasy till
> And add the halfpence to the pence

And prayer to shivering prayer, until
You have dried the marrow from the bone?
For men were born to pray and save:
Romantic Ireland's dead and gone,
It's with O'Leary in the grave.
   (Yeats,'September 1913')

 Both these poems emerge from personal experience. Yeats wrote 'September 1913' after the powerful businessman and owner of *The Irish Independent* newspaper, William M Murphy, publicly obstructed Yeats' attempt to get funding for an Art Gallery and who, with the support from the Catholic Church, ruthlessly suppressed the workers' great strike in Dublin in 1913. Whilst 'Conacre' may be interpreted as part of the wider political and cultural discourses on Northern Ireland, the poet's love for and unease with the rural landscape of his homeland is evident.
 Hewitt's power of description is exquisite in his nature poems. Yet even the rural landscape is political, drawn in context to the city left behind or to a history left even further behind. One can only conclude that for Hewitt, the aesthetic is always political. Nevertheless, consider the following description from 'East Antrim Winter'. One can feel the cold wet air, can almost smell the dark furrowed earth.

Wet roads between black hedges, and a sky
faint yellow-green with sunset, ribbed by trees
all stripped to twigs. Unregimented, loose,
rooks flap for home with slow and easy beat
from the dark furrows that this morning's plough
ripped over the bleached stubble.
   (from 'East Antrim Winter')

 Hewitt's love poems to his wife Roberta, his grandfather, his father and sister, are tender, lyrical and moving, and yet they are all tinged with pain and regret. In 'For Roberta In The Garden', Hewitt recalls that his wife was happiest when she was gardening 'kneeling on mould, a trowel in your glove', but that isn't enough for the poet. In the last two lines of this two-verse poem he writes, 'I wonder when you pause, you do not sing?/for such a moment surely has its song'. In 'I Lie Alone', Hewitt imagines his dead grandfather having come back to visit him as he sleeps in his old room. The poem is a whisper and one cannot but feel his emptiness and disappointment when he reaches his 'right hand out; no one was there'.
 There are few poems that can match the delicate gentleness of sibling love

as expressed in Hewitt's poem 'My Sister'. Even so, he still lets us glimpse his regret at not having a brother.

> And with the years her uses multiplied,
> Taught me, for instance, how to tie my shoe,
> And headed me by candlelight to bed,
> And only once reported when I lied.
> I should have liked a brother, it is true,
> But that was in addition, not instead.

In his poem 'An Irishman In Coventry', Hewitt describes the worst characteristic of Northern Irish intransigence. He uses the word 'our', owning the description as much as his fellow citizens.

> ...a people endlessly betrayed
> by our own weakness, by the wrongs we suffered
> in that long twilight over bog and glen,
> by force, by famine and by glittering fables
> which gave us martyrs when we needed men,
> by faith which had no charity to offer
> by poisoned memory, and by ready wit,
> with poverty corroded into malice,
> to hit and run and howl when it is hit.

Hewitt ends the poem with hope, believing that change is still possible.

> Yet like Lir's children banished to the waters
> Our hearts still listen for the landward bells.

Hewitt died in 1987 and sadly never witnessed the seismic changes to the political landscape in Ulster following the 1994 paramilitary ceasefires, which in turn heralded the power-sharing executive set out in the Good Friday Agreement in 1998. Hewitt had no wish to be an outsider in the country he loved deeply and considered his own. He lived out his last fifteen years in Belfast. Perhaps his dread of exile, physically and psychologically, was the very thing that charged his search for rootedness in his poetry. One wonders if for Hewitt, whose work explores the essence of the relationship between the social, political, physical and emotional elements of Northern Ireland, the aesthetic really was always political.

W. S. Milne

The Poetry of Norman MacCaig

Norman MacCaig (1910-1996) was of the distinguished generation of Scottish poets which included Hugh MacDiarmid, Sorley MacLean, Robert Garioch, Sydney Goodsir Smith, Edwin Morgan, Iain Crichton Smith, George Bruce, and George Campbell Hay. He published something like twenty books of poetry, starting with *Far Cry* in 1943 and finishing with *The Collected Poems* of 1993. His early career was as a schoolmaster, and his later as a Reader of Poetry at Stirling University. He won the Queen's Award for Poetry in 1985, and the Cholmondeley Award in 1975. Gordon Brown quoted from his poem 'Praise of a Man' at the funeral of Robin Cook in 2005:

> The beneficent lights dim
> but don't vanish.
> The razory edges
> dull, but still cut.
> He's gone:
> but you can see
> his tracks still, in the snow of the world.

He disavowed his first two books as obscure and meaningless, grounded, as he saw them to be, in the New Apocalypse school of poetry (the 'school' which included Dylan Thomas, Tom Scott, Maurice Lindsay, J F Hendry, Henry Treece, and W S Graham). He opted in the end, he says, for Apollonian rather than Dionysian energies. He found his own distinctive voice in his third volume, *Riding Lights* (1955), a book that has some affinities with The Movement, but embraces a vision all of MacCaig's own. From that book on he started to develop a classical compression and concision (he had studied Classics at Edinburgh University) lacking in the earlier volumes, leading to those qualities of accuracy, wit and clarity of seeing that we associate with his best work:

Wild Oats

> Every day I see from my window
> pigeons, up on a roof ledge – the males
> are wobbling gyroscopes of lust.

Last week a stranger joined them, a snowwhite
pouting fantail.
Mae West in the Women's Guild.
What becks, what croo-croos, what
demented pirhouetting, what a lack
of moustaches to stroke.

The females – no need to be one of them
to know
exactly what they were thinking – pretended
she wasn't there
and went on dowdily with whatever
pigeons do when they're knitting.

In his earlier work MacCaig relied heavily on a strict metricality, but later confessed that he found the writing of free verse of the order of excellence of 'Wild Oats' much harder. And I think one can see why. It is in the precise placing of the words that an exciting rhythm of perception is created, catching perceptions almost, as Kenneth Allott has argued, at the very point of their emergence. It is a hit-and-miss process, it must be confessed, as MacCaig himself acknowledged, involving no re-writing and the commitment of most poems to the waste-paper basket. It is a method of composition surely not to be recommended to students – an irony when one considers MacCaig's position as a Creative Fellow in poetry! However, it is a method which worked consummately for him. His most distinctive poem is what he terms 'a snapshot':

Praise of a Collie

She was a small dog, neat and fluid –
Even her conversation was tiny:
She greeted you with bow, never bow-wow.

Her sons stood monumentally over her
But did what she told them. Each grew grizzled
Till it seemed he was his own mother's grandfather.

Once, gathering sheep on a showery day,
I remarked how dry she was. Pollóchan said, 'Ah,
It would take a very accurate drop to hit Lassie.'

She sailed in the dinghy like a proper sea-dog.
Where's the burn? – she's first on the other side.
She flowed through fences like a piece of black wind.

But suddenly she was old and sick and crippled...
I grieved for Pollóchan when he took her a stroll
And put his gun to the back of her head.

I defy anyone to read that poem without a tear rising to their eye – what deeps of sympathy in a small compass! It is redolent of the best Greek epigrams or Celtic riddles (he is on record as admiring the 'extreme formality of Celtic art'). It is not simply a work of great craftsmanship, it is a work of great human imagination (in the re-working of the cliché 'sea-dog' so it is no longer a stock response, in the radiant image of 'a piece of black wind,' in the grace and dignity of Pollóchan and in the collie herself – and, finally, in the empathy of the narrator himself). 'Poetry involves order,' MacCaig has said, 'It has to submit to the control of the rational mind.' He agrees with Mallarmé who once replied to a lady who asked him, 'Do you not, then, ever weep in your poetry, Mons. Mallarmé?' 'No, madame,' he said, 'and I don't blow my nose in it either.' But that doesn't stop the reader crying if he wishes – as I did. This empathy with animals is reminiscent of the work of Henryson and Burns. 'What so pure,' MacCaig asks, 'As animals, /Each promise/Of new beginnings?'

As a poet MacCaig is not particularly interested in the transcendent (although, it has to be said, there are glimpses of something akin to it from time to time in his work). He is much more involved with the knowledge gained through 'the lust of looking' as he calls it, the apperceptions ('transparencies... Thickened to existence by my notice') gained through our 'five ports of knowledge':

In my eye I've no apple; every object
Enters in there with hands in pockets.
I welcome them all, just as they are,
Every one equal, none a stranger.

This is not completely true, of course, as he manages, like all fine poets, to transfigure, metamorphise, perpetually modify, these 'objects' into something strange and wonderful. A basking shark becomes 'That roomsized monster with a matchbox brain,' a toad crawls 'like a Japanese wrestler,' cows' muzzles are 'black and shiny as wet coal,' a haycart 'squats prickeared against the sky,' a goat is 'inquisitive as sin,/ White sarcasm walking, proof against surprise.' We see a 'heron, stiff/As a cruel clerk with gaunt writs in his hand' (a close reading of Dickens involved here, I suggest – Dickens was MacCaig's favourite author), 'An invisible drone boomed by/With a beetle in it,' 'straws like tame lightnings,' 'the mosses on the wall/Plump their fat cushions up,' 'a hen stares at nothing with one eye./Then picks it up' (that is the problem of the void taken care of then!), the grasshopper has a 'plated face' (one can see, or hear, already the armies stirring) and those male pigeons are 'wobbling gyroscopes of lust.' The effect, as Iain Crichton Smith has said, is like that of a conjuror drawing rabbits from a hat, 'infinity creatively renewed... Anyone who reads these poems without his or her eye sharpened must be blind.' And hooray to that! Although not taken in by D H Lawrence's vision of *Apocalpyse* (see his book of that title which was so influential for the New Apocalypse disciples), as some of his contemporaries had been, I do think MacCaig learned much from Lawrence's 'Birds, Beasts, and Flowers' poems – that strange affinity with the natural world one detects in both writers' work.

MacCaig possesses that rare gift of being able to bring the world to us anew, as if seen for the first time (in this, as some have rightly argued, he seems to prefigure in some ways Craig Raine's 'Martian' School of Poetry, although surely The Metaphysicals have some say in this too – see particularly MacCaig's 'The black cow is two native carriers/Bringing its belly home, slung from a pole.') This ability to merge dissimilar worlds, to reveal the interplay between the human and the non-human spheres, is a hallmark of MacCaig's work in general. An image of trees, their 'highborn heads tossing in the wind', or 'the airy skylark/Twittering like marbles squeezed in your fist' demonstrates the power, as Thomas Crawford has put it, to 'liken the natural scene to human artefacts or processes,' bringing original apperceptions into the world, finding likenesses in dissimilarity, as Aristotle argued true metaphor should, amalgamating the world's antinomies. So it is the poet brings us new images, fresh perceptions.

Such analysis would be too high-faluting for MacCaig, who is on record as saying 'I never met a White Goddess in my life and when I find myself in the company of singing robes, hieratic gestures and fluting voices I phone a taxi.' Such a stance keeps the poet's feet very much on the ground.

Outside of the startling image, MacCaig's poems focus on mortality and transience, the desert taking 'one slow step nearer', 'That heap of trash was once/A swan's throne,' 'And an evening full//Of the other evenings quietly began to die,' 'The sea makes a tired sound/That is always stopping though it never stops,' the poignant passing of love:

> Watching your face
> That makes an emptiness of this crowded place
> I stand not speaking, terrified to see
> You grown more lovely, and still lost to me.

Here we discover imagism renewed, minimalism perfected.

A sense of history's depredations is also never very far from the surface of a MacCaig poem, as in the surreal 'Whales that have learned to drown,/ Ballooning up, meet navies coming down' (notice the accuracy of 'ballooning,' so close to *baleen*, the horny plates of the whale obliquely summoning images of dreadnoughts), 'the implicated generations' as he expresses it in the poem 'Celtic Cross,' the compounding of violence and beauty:

> Under a ferocious snowfall
> of gulls and fulmars
> a corner of the bay is simmering
> with herring fry.
>
> Into them slice
> Assyrian hosts
> of mackerel...
>
> And in the gentle West
> a ladylike sunset
>
> swoons
> on the chaise-longue
> of the Hebrides.
>   (from 'Summer Idyll')

For MacCaig, man comprises (as for Hamlet) 'Frog and awkward angel,' 'louse and lion.' He is 'frantic with admiration/for the gray mess inside his skull,' tormented by an afterlife of his own devising – 'Sharp and hard,' he writes, 'the church still stands, barring the road to Hell' ('As if!' MacCaig seems to say, 'What rot!' 'What a lot of twaddle!' 'Nonsense!' – 'Silly hope' he calls it in another context). Nearer his true self is the Darwinian vision found in 'Clean in the mind, a new mind creeps into being,/Eating the old,' primeval slime preserved in what he terms 'the incorruptible lava of the word.' In the early poem 'Golden Calf' he asks, 'what/Mere human vocables you've ever heard... could overbear, I wonder,/the magniloquence of thunder?' Behind the Christian God then, for MacCaig, stands an even older, possibly crueller, Demiurge ('Creation's mad cross-purposes,' 'the cold adder... Curled round his neat and evil head.')

MacCaig was a conscientious objector in the Second World War, and his commitment to pacifism, his hatred of violence, is evident in much of his work:

> For five days and nights
> The windows have worn veils
> Of this water...
>
> My mind was like silence:
> An equivalence of peace.

The minor mode is illusive: there is great self-confidence here, an assured ability to oppose the strong of the world. The poet, in his own words, looks at the world 'through the wrong end of a telescope,' his imaginative lens focusing on the meagreness of what only appears mighty. So it is, viewed from a mountain-top, 'a great sailing ship, escaped/from the biggest bottle in the world,/glides grandly through the rustling water.' The tone sometimes is close to parable, as in small lochs' 'standing huge mountains on their watery heads.'

Obscurity to MacCaig's mind equates with 'bad art, bad manners'. There's much to be learned from that, and from what Roderick Watson has justly called his 'quiet and energised diction' (as in 'I nod and nod to my own shadow and thrust/A mountain down and down,' that seems to enact the very act of physical ascent itself). Iain Crichton Smith is MacCaig's most astute critic, and I will finish with some of his observations.

Smith has said that MacCaig is an observer dazzled by the world. His poetry, he says, 'will startle one with its way of seeing'; its 'invincible privacy' is at the same time 'exact and illuminating' like a modern Book of Hours. It is 'a well-made object with no excess luggage' showing an individual, independent spirit bent on discovering 'the thisness' of things. He calls him 'one of our finest poets' and I for one cannot disagree with him. Like Larkin, he hated fakery, pretence and embellishment, relying only on the power of language itself, 'the river building its sweet vocabulary/ toward the swarming languages of the sea.' He called himself 'a Zen-Calvinist.' Who can disagree when intellect and sensibility come together in such a fine unity?

W. S. Milne

The Poetry of Alexander Scott

It is an unfortunate fact of Scottish literary history that two of its finest poets share the same name: *Alexander Scott*. This can lead to some confusion. The sixteenth century poet (c.1520-c.1590) is well known enough, especially for his love lyrics, and has been comprehensively anthologised. His twentieth century counterpart (1920-1989) is, however, less well known (he does not appear, for example, in Robert Crawford and Mick Imlah's *The New Penguin Book of Scottish Verse,* published in 2000, although there are four poems by the Renaissance poet there). It is with the later Alexander Scott that I am concerned in this short essay.

Scott published seven books of poetry in his lifetime: *The Latest in Elegies,* 1949; *Selected Poems,* 1950; *Mouth Music. Poems and Diversions,* 1954; *Cantrips,* 1968; *Greek Fire. A Sequence of Poems,* 1971; *Double Agent: Poems in Scots and English,* 1972; and *Selected Poems 1943-1974,* 1975 — all of which should be better known than they are. Scott was an Aberdonian who was instrumental in the struggle to create the first Department of Scottish Literature to exist in Scotland, established in the academic year 1971-2 at the University of Glasgow where he was both tutor and reader in Scottish Literature. Although he wrote some verse in English, his first commitment was to the Scots language, and it is with his Scots poems that I deal solely here.

Scott is one of the finest Scottish makars of the twentieth century, with an ear keen and alert to the language's natural idioms, far removed from the formal stiffness you occasionally find in some of the Modern Renaissance poets such as Alice V. Stuart, Edith Anne Robertson and Douglas Young, for example. (The great exception to this, of course, is the poetry of Hugh MacDiarmid, although it has to be admitted that even there the fault is often discoverable.) As a scholar deeply immersed in Scottish language and literature, Scott consciously avoids what he calls 'dictionary-dredging exercises' ('a sort of mortuary' for some Scottish poets as Norman MacCaig terms it), relying more on the living flow of speech:

> Winter the warld, albeid the winnock-pane
>   Has flouers o frost as bricht as spring's.
> The clouds the sea-maws scour are kirkyaird stane,
> Gray and cauld and lourd on skaichan wings.

> The peerie birds in ilka naukit tree,
> Quaet they sit as cones o fir.
> Langsyne they skimmed the lift, stravaigan free,
> But grippit in winter's neive they canna stir.

Scott's speech-base is the North-East *koiné*, its starkness, physicality, its 'harsh strength' as Lorna Macintyre has described it, especially that of urban Aberdeen, welded to emphatic Anglo-Saxon and Hopkinsian alliterative rhythms. (His translation of the Anglo-Saxon *The Seafarer* into Scots is the equal of Ezra Pound's much better known version, in my opinion.)[1] 'Scots is at its least diluted in the North-East: written and spoken Doric do not seriously diverge from one another' Tom Hubbard has written (on Scott's poetry, in his essay 'Reintegrated Scots: The Post MacDiarmid Makars'), following what Scott himself calls 'the principal highway' of 'colloquially-based Scots':

> The sea-maw spires i the stane-gray lift
> Owre sworlan swaws o the stane-gray sea,
> Flaffers her wings —a flash o faem-white feathers—
> And warssles awa i the wake o the trauchled trawler
> That hirples hame hauf-drouned wi the wecht o herrin.

(These lines are from 'Heart of Stone,' a long poem commissioned by BBC Television and broadcast on 2 January 1966. Tom Scott wrote of this poem, rightly I think, that in it, at last, Scotland had found again 'a poetry that begins to look like the great physical poetry of Gavin Douglas.')

Beside this element of strong physical articulation, George Bruce detects, again I think rightly, that there is a deep 'implication of community' in Alexander Scott's work, discovering there a poetry which concentrates on those principles of language which unite rather than divide people, a 'living speech' (as Leonard Mason calls it) which looks back to, and takes its strength from, the Medieval Makars —particularly from the poetry of William Dunbar and Gavin Douglas— re-establishing the force of rhetoric in Scottish verse:

> Reid river rinnan through my flesh,
>   Your spring is far, sae far
> That I micht skaich owre aa the warld

---

[1] It is interesting to note that the Orkneyan poet, George Mackay Brown, who studied literature at the University of Aberdeen, also learned much from Anglo-Saxon literature and from Hopkins (he wrote his Ph.D on Hopkins' poetry) but chose to write his poems and stories in English rather than in dialect.

And scran in ilka star
And never see the dernit source
That drives frae whaur, frae whaur?...

But douts are straes to sic a stream
That caresna whence it's run,
And whether endin fins the faem
Or sinks in sandy grun,
Atween twa nichts, o birth and death,
Your burn shines back the sun.

The melding of craft and intellect here overcomes the naïveté, the sentimentality, of much of the Kailyard poetry that preceded Scott, those rhymesters (with their chiming, mawkish 'crambo-clink' as Burns so disparagingly termed it) who give little or no thought to technique or content in their writing. His verse carries, with contemporary conviction, the temper and strength of the Scots tongue, as it did once in the tales of Sir Walter Scott and Robert Louis Stevenson, avoiding what George Bruce calls 'couthy sentiment' (that is, 'easy, shallow feeling').

It is the 'makar's standard o sang,' his 'skeelie science,' 'the weave of human brains' (as Scott himself terms it) that the true poet follows in his making, his craft — the ancient and abiding Scottish word 'makar' hewing close to the original Greek meaning of poiesis. As Stravinsky has said (in the first chapter of his *Poetics of Music*) 'the verb *poiein* from which the word is derived means nothing else but *to do* or *to make*.' It is the true poet's duty or burden ('darg' as Scott calls it) to make language dance and sing out of the mundane materials of everyday life, even though, as Karl Barth (in his Commentary on *The Epistle to the Romans*) has argued: 'my noblest capacity becomes my deepest perplexity; my noblest opportunity, my uttermost distress; my noblest gift, my darkest menace':

But I'm no great eneuch, and sae my lack
Maun serve, for gin my hert has little knack
For haudden the warld's rowth, and gin my sicht
Just glisks on beauty, still there's sangs to mak
That only loss alane can sing aricht
   (Gin loss be great eneuch).

And so it is Scott's 'skill as a master craftsman' (the words are Leonard Mason's) find their truest expression perhaps in the elegiac form, as in his great 'Coronach (For the Dead of the 5/7 Battalion, The Gordon Highlanders)':

Waement the deid
I never did,
Ower gled I was ane o the lave
That someway baid alive
Tae trauchle my thowless hert
Wi ithers' hurt...

Waement the deid
I never did,
But nou I am safe awa
I hear their wae
Greetan greetan dark and daw
Till I their biddin dae.

(War's bravery is praised —not so often hymned in modern times— in a humble fashion here. The poet makes no play of the fact that he himself was awarded the Military Cross for bravery in action in the Second World War.)

Norman MacCaig writes also of the 'tenderness' to be found in Scott's elegies to Jayne Mansfield and Marilyn Monroe, a softness at times hidden beneath a 'tough and sardonic manner'. It is, as one critic has said, the 'underlying humanity... his warmth and irony' which impresses here, and another of 'the pity mingled with anger and admiration... undermining pretension, exposing hypocrisy and hammering home the painful ironies of modern life.' This tender compassion, combined sometimes with a harsh irony, reminds one at times of his earlier namesake's love lyrics:

She lies ablow my body's lust and love,
A country dearly-kent, and yet sae fremd
That she's at aince thon Tir-nan-Og I've dreamed,
The airt I've lived in, whaur I mean to live,
And mair, much mair, a mixter-maxter warld
Whaur fact and dream are taigled up and snorled.

I ken ilk bay o aa her body's strand,
Yet ken them new ilk time I come to shore,
For she's the uncharted sea whaur I maun fare
To find anither undiscovered land,
To find it fremd, and yet to find it dear,
To seek it aye, and aye be bidan there.

One can detect the influence of Donne's metaphysics here – it is just as well to remember, perhaps, that widespread interest in Donne's poetry was revived in the early twentieth century by Herbert Grierson in his Gifford Lectures, delivered whilst he was Professor of English Literature at Aberdeen University, a revival usually attributed to T. S. Eliot. (The echo of Hamlet's' well-known sexual pun on the word 'country' is clear enough here also.)

Scott's satire on Calvinism carries a similar force:

> A hunder pipers canna blaw
>   Our trauchled times awa,
> Drams canna droun them out, nor sang
> Hap their scarecrow heids for lang.
>
> Gin aa the warld was bleezan fou,
>   What gowk wad steer the plou?
> Gin chiels were cowpan quines aa day
> They'd mak (but fail to gaither) hay.
>
> Pit by your bagpipes, brak your gless,
>   Wi quines, keep aff the gress,
> The-day ye need a hert and harns
> As dour as the diamant, cauld as the starns.

This is Scott's 'take' on the modern 'unco guid' that Burns savaged so mercilessly in his 'Holy Willie's Prayer':

> O Thou that in the Heavens does dwell,
> Wha, as it pleases best Thysel,
> Sends ane to Heaven an' ten to Hell
>   A' for Thy glory,
> And no for onie guid or ill
>   They've done before Thee!

Like Burns, Scott also saw that the eighteenth century Edinburgh poet Robert Fergusson (see his 'Letter to Robert Fergusson') was a possible model to emulate for the forging of wit, humour, satire and irony within the context of vernacular verse (demanding what Leonard Mason calls 'a pride in what is good in native achievement') situating his 'hameil lays' (his 'native-born songs') within a European tradition (but not slavishly), and celebrating what is best in Scottish culture and tradition (see particularly Scott's poem on Byron, perhaps the most famous of all Aberdonians). Scott thinks that for too long the Scots have been blind to what is both best and rich in their own history, a concern he shares with the modern Edinburgh poet Robert Garioch. So it is that he is keen on the act of translating, and of translating especially out of the Gaelic stream in Scottish literature (he has translated many of the poems of Derick Thomson, for instance).

Scott then is 'of the company of auld makars' (as Leonard Mason phrases it) retaining an involvement with a community far removed from the trivia of modern communications, writing a poetry universal in its implications — not clannish, not parochial, not sentimental, always lurking dangers for dialect poets. As Walter Keir has written, in Scott's work we see 'traditional forms coming to terms with modern materials,' and achieving what Leonard Mason calls 'a creative synthesis of the old and the new.' His poetry is not predictable, not repetitive, but is crafted to perfection. It instantiates a personal voice which stands out against an age of impersonal utterance. 'Heart of Stone' is his masterpiece, his masterwork:

> Frae clintie seas and bens as coorse as brine
> For fowk sae fit to daur the dunt o storms
> Wi faces stobbed by the stang o saut
> Or callered by country winds
> In a teuch toun whaur even the strand maks siller,
> Rugged frae the iron faem and the stanie swaws
> As the sweel o the same saut tide
> Clanjamfries crans and kirks by thrang causeys
> Whaur cushat's croudle mells wi sea-maw's skirl,
> And hirplan hame hauf-drouned wi the wecht o herrin
> The trauchled trawler waffs in her wake
> A flaffer o wings – a flash o faem-white feathers –
> As the sea-maw spires i the stane-gray lift
> Owre sworlan swaws o the stane-gray sea
> And sclents ti the sea-gray toun, the hert o stane.

Alexander Scott's verse is like a burn that 'shines back the sun,' and holds its own with other fine North-East makars such as Lord Byron, Arthur Johnston, Charles Murray, Violet Jacob, Helen B. Cruickshank, and Flora Garry. His work is distinctly Scottish in its stress on 'making.' But this is only part of the truth. Like the great Scottish philosopher David Hume, the makar must emphatically know that reason is always the servant of the passions. And so it is in Alexander Scott's poetry —where we see a man who, as well as being a master of his craft, is one who also feels the world deeply:

The fire burns laich,
The clock wins roun to twal,
  And I maun dwall
  Alane, and dreich.

My love is taen,
I hae the dark for bride,
  And I maun bide
  Dreich, and alane.

John F. Deane

Semibreve

I sat, in the island chapel, moor's edge, winter;
winds groaned and chistled round the walls outside,
the timbers creaked in the afterwarmth,

ghosts from the quenching slipped up through the rafters;
there was a souring emptiness though I sat entranced
by sacrament and my own minuscule being – when the walls

whispered – *Listen!* There was no-one. There was nothing.
Even the winds had died. And the chill winterlight
had dimmed. But a tiny chime had happened, vibrated

on my inner listening. The tiniest hint of spittle
tipped against my brow but there was nothing when I wiped
my hand across it. The door moaned again, a sudden breeze

forcing it and I stood, watchful, and shaken. That
was the first semibreve sounded of a gifted music.
I am day and night now, listening. Tuned for it, and waiting.

Tuning

He was up in the choir-loft, tuning the pipes
of the old century's wind-pump organ; I heard
taps and bangs on metal, the strangest half-throated
off-notes, near-notes, puffs and sighs and cough-blasts;

and then he was playing – Bach, Buxtehude, Peters –
and it was a young Jehovah's making, a bright hands-full
sailing over oceans of soul-light, filling the chill of the chapel
with a lush of breathing. Now, in my everyday listening,

for the poem, the music, I am Mary before the ash-soft fall
of the messenger, I am John after the disappearance
beyond the clouds; I listen to the silence beyond the thuck
and thudding of a day's importance, to hear the hum that figures

countryside darkness, the sounds of April
whispering over into May, the thunder of apple blossoms
dropping from the tree; I listen for the tune that my days make
in the workings of love, in the notes' approximations to a symphony.

Sheenagh Pugh

The Eye

Across the bay, they're building a house
with a glass wall, panes all the way up

into the gable, windows that wrap
around corners for a view as wide

as sea and sky, to take in Sumburgh Head,
Auriga, every passing vessel

and pod of orca, storm-force gales,
anvil clouds, the cliffs of Levenwick,

the waxing moon lighting a track
clear to Fair Isle. This huge eye,

lidless, unfillable, as hungry
for every last object it can rest on

as if it were mortal, knowing how soon
light goes by; how little time it has.

Graham Hardie

A man alone searching for the white narwhale

I pick the cards for Uist
And they are The Hermit and The Moon;
A man alone searching for the white narwhale
Along the shingled sand,
Where the doves of Iona fly overhead
And the maidens of Rum,
Dance and take his rough hand,
And show him the unsettled waters of darkness
In the plight of words unsaid,
And the parasite in the soul of man.

The Harris Lady

To Oana,
The Harris lady
Of the dream of dolphins
And salty water.

To Oana,
The musical monk
Of the switchblade
And the tiresome fold.

To Oana,
The light beheld
By guides of snow
In winter shallows,
And water cold.

Rosalind Hudis

Ancestral Litany

not of faces so much – but hands.
My gran's, for instance, sunk
to the wrist in a swamp of flour
and egg, or eel dim under water
while she skinned potatoes.

Hands on duty – I'd catch
her thumb's intricate, flashed
speed as it forced the peeler,
like a diver unhooking the welded
corsets of a wreck.

The back of her head, then,
but if she'd turned sometimes
to mind me, I don't remember it.
I was waiting for her to raise
each potato, nude and wet,

to the light, her fingers
raw-puckered and somehow
like survivors of injury.
And what hits now is the clang
shut of talk. The make-do

and bury of those hands, even
off duty, to impress me,
unravelling the toughened
skins of coxes in one silent
sleight of knife.

Cheap Pianos

come and go
like marriages – the brief
heady ones balancing
a sediment of whisky
in a re-used tumbler
at the end, or the keys
stress-cracks have inched up,
like party nails eroding
weeks after the event.

We kept one
for its *fin-de-siècle* inlay,
its candle-holders mottled
with vintage wax,
an old queen, feathered
by echoes of gas-lit bawdy.
It played a boozed,
coquettish slide around
the sex of a harmony.

Another seemed too stern
for its small iron bones,
all black-stained mahogany
thick as scripture. We'd humped it
from a dank chapel, unprayed in
for years. It took five
good men to raise, but its rhetoric
was nearly gone - mothy
and thinned as an old heart.

I thought of the duty of voices
suited, gathered in
from the last farms
beyond electricity, the echo
and cannon of them
in the chromatic sunlight,
how they might seep between
the piano's staves of wood
and wire, their pitch blurring.

R.V. Bailey

Tom Tiddler's Ground

(Brewer: 'a place where it is easy to pick up a
fortune, or to make a place in the world for oneself'.
Cf. the children's game – 'Here we are on Tom
Tiddler's Ground, picking up gold and silver'.)

Like El Dorado
Does not occur
On any map. Those

Who go there
Don't go alone,
Are there already, though

They won't know this
Until they arrive.
A midsummer place,

Where evidence, data,
Tidemark and footprint –
Absent Without Leave.

Drill of woodpecker, bark
Of fox more accurate gauge
Than metronome or rule.

Territory of the clown,
Whose smile is heartbreak,
Where here and there

And then and now
Shake hands
Before they part.

Robert Stein

Mette Von O

She sits as usual in a corner of the chair,
One tiny dress-button gone.
She says nothing mostly or bites her lip
And must recover simply by being there.

And of this expensive silence and his respectful head,
The dark patterned carpet,
The brass lamp and the masks
She smiled once and nearly said ...

When a lamp goes off or I am late
It means I love you.
She might say anything to his cocked ear.
Her stocking is snagged by a splinter on the chair.

If he might speak, he would confess to paint her
Splayed out in sleep as on a crucifix,
Or drowning forever through leagues of the sea;
But he says nothing and remains in his chair.

Tonight, The Dead

Tonight all the dead are drifting
Down towards earth. An armada of loves
Winnowed and sighing.

In the hesitations of the evening
The dead are coming,
In the yesterdays of the ocean
Spending its waves,
And in the still star-clusters
They are falling.

Tonight all the dead are coming down.
In the tapping of rain,
In the shivering of trees -
The dust drifts back
From the silent places.

Tim Cresswell

Possible Pubs

meet me
                at the rush and shiver
take me
                to the pat and tap
meet me
                at the pluck and quiver
take me
                to the trick and clap
seek me
                by the curve and flutter
find me
                in the wince and snide
seek me
                by the trust and stutter
find me
                in the pulse and slide
see me
                at the luck and couple
join me
                near the kiss and skew
see me
                at the curse and suckle
join me
                near the wreck and screw
hold me
                in the wrench and scare
drink with me love
                drink with me there

Mandy Pannett

Tales from the Sculpture Park

Who is this striding out of the forest
urgent and zealous with news
of a scoop? If he was human
he'd tread on the celandines –
if he was real, not rock.

I loop with a path
to the bluebell wood where a silver
carapace shines in the sun and two great boulders
are giants in love, so close
they almost could kiss.

Deeper in, it's cold:
the wolf has his sniper-eye fixed on a sheep,
a headless Ganesha approves.

This must be
where the Wild Hunt stopped
one blackthorn winter to set down its dead –

Yet there's spring in this clearing, a reason
for yellow and they are still here, these symbols,
these clues – clear as the sparrows
but hidden by leaves.

There are bulletins here for a man in a hurry
and ladders of glass to the sky.

William Bedford

Pillar Box Farm

They called it Pillar Box Farm.
The postman didn't know when the pillar box
was fixed in the wall. 1840s he reckoned,
when the post began. Before his time anyway.
I might have guessed that without being told
just by looking at the old photographs.
But he was joking. Passing the time.

In the photographs, a horse grazes.
There is a reek of stack yard and silage
rising from the cold celluloid.
Chickens peck at the verges.
I can see my grandmother's strong arms,
the smoke from grandfather's pipe.
A sheep dog watches us from the hedge
in case I try to walk into the picture.
The gold lettering on the carrier cart
says *John Bedford: farmer.*
My family name etched into timeless sunlight.

Sheep-washing

We washed 'em every spring he said,
leaning on the wash dyke bridge
to see the water-forget-me-nots,
racing underneath the wooden slats.
Since he was a lad, they'd done it that way.
Before that too I shouldn't wonder.
Five shillings per hundred sheep:
the same every season:
the end of winter, the beginning of spring.
You might know he was recalling spring
the way his eyes unblinkered.
Five shillings per hundred sheep . . .
in case I hadn't heard him right . . .
and a cup of tea for the quickest lads,
the first to get the sheep into the river.
It was always a Manor Farm treat,
something they did that had been done before.

I heard about it from my grandfather.
He worked the farms here too,
though left in the war and never came back.
I've got a photograph of him when he was two,
sitting on his father's knee in the trap,
the horse lapping the cold water,
thigh deep in the shallow ford.
He'd be the kind of boy who'd win the cup of tea.
I don't suppose there were rams? I asked.
You suppose right, lad. We weren't daft.
You could break a leg, messing with rams.
They turn nasty when they feel cornered.
I feel cornered, and turn away.
I watch the forget-me-nots,
dancing in the water like my grandfather.
The sheep were enough for the lads.
The farmer dealt with the rams.

Jennifer A. McGowan

Sounding

A turbulent season.
The waves uneven, cross-angled, fretful.
He fights for balance.

A day off means more than no income.
It means weakness, defeat, acknowledgment
that the sea is angry and tired.
Still a certainty, yes, but an empty one.

Insistent chink
of the rosary against the wheel:
relict of faith and the bishop's blessing.
A long time since he's bent his knee
but the tinny crucifix
is stubborn, will not break.
He remembers the soft fragility
of his grandmother's hand
before First Communion;
later, his wife kneeling by a stone.
As much for that
as for anything,
he closes his eyes, mumbles a half-phrase.

Nothing happens. He back-throttles,
checking the LORAN. Goes to set a last line,
needing something to run deep.
Staring up, he wrestles with the gathering clouds.
Whispers a name. Takes a jagged breath.

The whitebait boil to the surface.

Ed Reiss

'Pitch me *vox clamans*' :
Geoffrey Hill's *Odi Barbare* (Clutag Press, 2012)

At first reading, Geoffrey Hill's latest publication, *Odi Barbare*, is neither hospitable nor pretty. Hill likens some of his recent work to that of Anselm Kiefer: 'iron spikes sticking up out of a blasted landscape'. With its ellipses, inversions and mangled syntax, its lines set in deliberate disrelation one to another, its dissent from the consensus of contemporary poetry, *Odi Barbare* will strike many readers as being both odious and barbarous.

For all that, it is a wonderful and wonderfully strange book. Hill has described himself (on *Newsnight*) as 'a kind of rip-roaring fantasist' who likes 'getting onto a bench and standing on one leg, figuratively speaking.' He moves in these new Odes through phantasmagoria and phanopoeia – 'Dead balloonists over the Niger Delta / Skywriting *Freedom*' and 'salvation's voyager cone alighting / Briefly on Pendle' – to moments of scraggy epiphany:

> Blowy fieldbanks haggarded with narcissi,
> Fells that change colour as the sunlight strengthens.

The odes are 'haggarded' with such lines, apparently the product of direct observation and in which the intellectually surprising word ('haggarded') is also surprisingly right. Some of Hill's descriptions of Nature double as observations on his own poetry.

> Bracken-guarded airfields where now the pigeons
> Ponderous, wing-laden, in near-botched take-offs,
>   Rattle the spinneys.

The 'near-botched take-offs' could also refer to Hill's adventures with the Sapphic line itself. The Sapphic is a Greek metre, adapted by the Latin poets (notably Horace) and then adopted by such English poets as Philip Sidney, William Cowper and Isaac Watts. (Hill has speculated that the Sapphic appeals to Calvinists because of its inexorability.) The form was used by Tennyson and Swinburne; by Ezra Pound and, more recently, by Marilyn Hacker.

The Sapphic line – on which, more later – has a reputation for being foreign or barbarous to the English tongue, because it does not, on the whole, mimic or reproduce the rhythms of the English speaking voice, as iambic pentameter, for instance, can. Perhaps that is what attracts Geoffrey Hill to it. In his *Odi Barbare*, the Sapphic line is the main character, or what gives the book its character. In its 52 odes, each line kicks off with a strong stress; and, whilst this is difficult to sustain, it can be turned to immediate effect. Note, for instance, how the stanza below lands on and springs off Hill's portmanteau-word 'jelk':

> Assegais whish-washed in the fleshy Empire
> Jelk you inside out like a dumdum bullet;

'Jelk' here combines 'jerk' and 'squelch', so that the English verb imitates the Zulu noun for their stabbing-spear, the *iklwa* or *ixwa*, so called for the sucking sound it made when withdrawn from the enemy's flesh. At his best, Geoffrey Hill can 'jelk you inside out'.

Let me now take some jelks at identifying the preoccupations of *Odi Barbare*. They are brief provisional jelks for, as Donald Hall remarked over a quarter of a century ago, 'Hill's quick alternations of tone, his sudden and frequent reverses, work to prevent paraphrase; no sooner does the reader think he has accomplished paraphrase than he realizes that he has allowed a counter-thrust to escape notation. We may as well summarise a Beethoven quartet.' What goes for the part is true too for the whole. That said, I would hazard that among the Odes' main themes are: wisdom; despair; depths of memory; injustice; the fate of the soul (specifically Hill's soul); and 'prophecy's tunnel vision' in an age of 'plutocratic anarchy'. Of course, one could make a different list and include poetry, beauty, folly and love. The odes address both World Wars and the Holocaust. Tudor statecraft also impinges. Geographically, the poems range between Italy, Israel, India, Poland, Africa and Wales. Should this be confusing, then recall what Hill told *The Economist*. 'If they say this poem is difficult because we cannot grasp a coherent point of view, I would say, "well, neither can I. And this poem is part of the dramatization of that." A lot of my poems are about failing to get something, or failing to be able to clear one's meaning finally. And I think that's a perfectly legitimate area to write in; provided one is technically efficient and ends up with something beautiful.'

Whatever the main subject, the reader will be struck by the scope and span of Hill's imagination, dancing as it does from 'Cuban rumba' to Yiddish *broyges tants* to 'a shuffled stepdance'. Drawing on film, novels, painting and music, these odes are populated by saints, statesmen, philosophers, artists, writers and mythical and fictional characters. Among the poets referenced are Horace, Dante and Petrarch; Carducci and Tagore; Wyatt, Herbert and Milton; Blake and Hopkins; Yeats, Eliot and Pound; Wallace Stevens and

Ivor Gurney. Though readers won't be astonished to find such Hillian heroes as John Ruskin and Hannah Arendt, they may be surprised to meet 'Nitro Glisserinski the anarchist with / Nitra his daughter'. And whilst some stanzas are conspicuously abstract, others are enlivened by physical surprises, not least the Pompidou Centre, 'Vulgar Corpus clock with its nasty locust' and 'the seventeen arched / Accrington Town viaduct'.

Along with the weighty sense of 'words as their own tribunal', there is the fun and inventiveness of Hill's lexis, with its archaism ('maugre'); its resurrections of the obsolete ('wakeman'); its poeticism ('lave'); its rare words ('glimmerous' and 'uncomfort'); its macaronic forays into Hebrew, Latin, Italian, French, Yiddish and German; and its scattering of grace-words not to be found in the OED, such as 'throp', 'clarimote', 'prankdom' and 'affrontage'. Hill hops from oligarchic Globish ('biznis' and 'state-of-art project') to pastoral Classicism ('Heaving lyre-pronged heads from hoof-podged Clitumnus'); from styptic Graeco-Latinate ('Such the free topoi absolution's finis'), through the Biblical ('while he was yet afar off') to slang ('Man, who ya tellin?'). Meanings are conflated in 'a spillaged sheikhdom', where that 'spillaged' conveys both the image of an oil spillage and the sound of 'pillaged'. And rhetorical figures figure ingeniously; for instance the two lines – 'What we can't say we can't say. Can't say we can / *Whistle it either*' – play with antanaclasis, anadiplosis and antimetabole.

Pleasures of surprise are joined by those of familiarity. Hill continues his love-affair with the hyphen. In Ode XII alone we find 'bronze-putteed', 'midday-lit', 'clock-time', 'well-hackled', 'horse-/collared', 'Child-steps', 'self-found', 'grey-coppery', 'sun-shot', 'Barely-heard'. The 'self-found' is also found in a list of self-compounds: 'self-willing', 'self-enthralling', 'self-hounding', 'self-gathered', 'self-hazard', 'selfhood', 'self-fulfilling', 'self-wronging' and 'unself-stabilizing'. Other prefixes intimate his belief in the Fall, that 'aboriginal calamity' which also infects language ('ill-fictioned', 'ill-endowed', 'disrooted' and 'befoundered') and is traceable in Hill's mis-compounds: 'mispride', 'mishandled', 'misfestive', 'miscreant', 'misunderstanding', 'misanthropist', 'mis-/Spoken' and 'misadventure'.

Apart from its incidental and local detail, what of the collection as a whole? It has been claimed that the Sapphic form is misaligned with, or athwart to, the genius of the English tongue. The success of *Odi Barbare*, however, turns on how Hill tackles this mismatch. Does he manage to work with, and against, his awkward metric? Can he sustain the sequence to 'blast access to unsuspected / caverns of fluorspar'?

To answer this requires further consideration of Hill's technical daimon, the Sapphic line itself. Each of the fifty two odes has six quatrains; and each quatrain is composed of three longer lines and one shorter one. In its strong form, towards which Hill tends, each longer Sapphic line demands seven stresses out of a possible eleven. The metrical feet are arranged: trochee, spondee, dactyl, trochee, spondee. Then the shorter line, concluding the quatrain, is in the form: dactyl, spondee.

That calls for many-stressed, spiked, inspissate lines:

> Cast in their own sakes, let be blackthorn, whitethorn,
> Branches fisting twigtight new-knuckled well-stubbed
> Starry! – Purcell's burgeoning bass chaconies
>   Stressed and in order.

Whilst this may be achieved in one twigtight stanza, to sustain it over 312 stanzas and 1248 lines is daunting, partly because the English language relies on small, unstressed words such as articles and prepositions, to oil the wheels and keep its train of thought running. In practice, the Sapphic line often falls short of its ideal or strong form: one of the spondees can be replaced with a trochee, or if they both are, then the line will sound more like trochee, trochee, dactyl, trochee, trochee. In other words it can approximate to a trochaic pentameter with a little dactylic skip in the middle.

We don't speak in Sapphics. The measure doesn't suit the norms of either spoken or written English. So to compose in them at any length is to risk losing the cadences and inflections of everyday speech, the warmth, fluency and suppleness of a speaking voice. Recognisably human rhythms, responding and adjusting to recognisable imaginative context, may be outdrowned by the 'harsh cryings' of the quasi-robotic, an 'in-/Human poetics', 'stilted', 'Rhetoric uptight', like an ugly auto-translation. Hill takes the gamble, intrinsic in the form, of becoming 'radically, irretrievably, alienated'. Avoiding accessibility and 'desirable features of conversation', he is prepared to sound 'cricked', refractory, 'not urbane'. Often he is writing under the signs of both Hopkins and Pound, 'not doting on mellifluousness', wanting 'Something wrought more telling than melopoeia', where melopoeia is Pound's term for 'the musical and rhythmic qualities of poetic language', (as opposed to, or complemented by, logopoeia, 'the dance of the intellect among words'). Some of Hill's lines acknowledge the stresses of their metric: 'Must I pump more stresses as you command me?' And some stanzas seem to be anticipating and pre-empting criticism, by incorporating it.

> Something sprung here that you may well recoil from.
> Stick with hazardous enigmatic fractured
> Metaphysics' laboured accommodation
>   Unrecommended.

Alienating and de-automatising, the very artificiality of the Sapphic metre in English works against 'tone' where 'tone', according to Hill, 'is what people expect and suppose themselves familiar with'. If iambic pentameter is the fertile, populous valley of English poetry, then Sapphics would be the desert from which Hill pitches his *vox clamans*.

Estranged from familiar rhythms, the reader must decide whether to speak lines 'conversationally', or sound them out according to their Sapphic measure. Consider the short line: 'So there you have me'. Colloquially we might stress the word 'there'. But as a Sapphic (Adonic), a dactyl and a spondee, the emphasis will fall on the first word and the last two, giving a quite different meaning. Again, in the line 'All that's beyond me', we would normally stress the word 'that's'. But the Sapphic guides us to stress the words 'All' and 'me', as well as the second syllable in 'beyond'. So instead of a shoulder-shrug ('All that stuff is too difficult for me'), we are pointed towards an objective infinite ('everything which is outside of my ego'). Take another example: 'weep not to hear them' would, read conversationally, be an injunction against weeping. Read Sapphically, however, the second word, 'not', is unstressed; and we are enjoined to weep for what we cannot hear. So 'Metric makes gnomic' and, in setting up 'cross-rhythms', metric makes ambiguous.

Metric can also clarify, by indicating, for instance, where the caesura falls. Consider the end of the twelfth ode, with its unusual enjambment between stanzas, its 'Apotheosis'

>As of bare hedges as of fields awash, light
>Clouds I call grey-coppery early mornings
>Fused with sun-shot fog and the grassblades crispy
>>Barely-heard tinsel.

Here the Sapphic framework encourages us to pause in the first line after the word 'hedges' and in the third line after the word 'fog'. 'Fused' at the start of that line asks for a stronger stress than we might normally give it; and the word 'I' in line 2 declines emphasis. Again, in the following lines, the pause comes before the little skip of two weak syllables: the words 'one hears of' all take a stress; and I suggest that in 'Neck and chin bleeding' only the conjunction 'and' passes unstressed.

>Things that one hears of like the violinist's
>Neck and chin bleeding from an all-extorting
>>Final cadenza.

Because the (strong) Sapphic line both starts and ends with a trochee followed by a spondee, this allows symmetry of repetition, which Hill draws on twice: 'Zephaniah, Benjamin Zephaniah,' or '*Hannah Arendt*, heard you say. Hannah Arendt'. (The second example plays on the palindrome of 'Hannah'.)

In its strong form, the Sapphic line is front-loaded with stresses. The line starts with four stresses out of a possible five. (Only the second position is unstressed.) Keeping this in mind can create a more insistent effect than if the lines were spoken without regard for their formal measure. Ponder the following examples: they are all beginnings of lines which have been truncated to illustrate the point. In every case, I would contend, both the first and each of the last three words given should take its full and rightful stress.

> If the soul so glares
> No, not wrong bride, wronged
> Now am too far in.
> Cresting those flash webs
> Breathe on my nesh eyes
> Broken that first kiss
> Paolo I am not

When a hyphenated word is involved, this means stressing each part of the compound-word equally:

> Take these strange-willed odes
> Giving song hearth-room

Since the strong Sapphic ends with a spondee, this too should be sounded, as in 'Nominating Israel here as rogue state', or 'Trailing their long screams'.

The second ode warns of 'Rumpus, uncouth anacolutha, bullish/ Metamorphs treading out a line'. The bull here might be a friendly nod to his ex-colleague Christopher Ricks, who compared Hill's comedy on one occasion to 'that of a bull, an Irish Bull'. The anacolutha refers to lack of grammatical sequence, or 'the passing from one construction to another before the former is completed'. 'Uncouth anacoluthon' is a phrase Hill has used of the turn – 'Enough! the Resurrection' – in Hopkins' poem 'That Nature is a Heraclitean Fire and of the comfort of the Resurrection'. After many readings, the bullish 'treading out' lightens and seems less recalcitrant. As it fades, the delicacy of Hill's writing emerges. The stanzas can indeed be seen as 'wings and altars / Love's hieroglyphics'.

The difficulties of *Odi Barbare* include problems of word-order, omissions and punctuation. In order to meet the rhythm – or for other reasons — Hill makes strange word-choices and inverts word-order, convolutes his clauses, obscuring how the sentence is constructed: what is subject, verb and object, if indeed the sentence has them. Sometimes rhythm seems to over-ride sense, at the expense of clarity and fluency, the result being, like Hopkins and the great works of modernism, 'repulsive to the settled taste of the time'. Some lines — such as 'Terms at law viz *Tragedy Anticommons*' — read like a crib-sheet or 'merest memo'. Some — 'Titan arum's rotten Sumatran splendour', or 'Logics purport twisted to sport of purpose' — look like cryptic crossword clues. Several seem, or indeed are, inchoate, 'tense with the bafflements of communication'. One could bet on what lines might be cited by MacSikker et al. in their hostile reviews. Could it be 'Tacitus self-willing the Imperator'; 'Passive agon gravity's apatheia'; 'Accolade Muses' dithyrambics far-fraught'; or 'What you damn well care then bestowing credence?'? Some of these gobbets might be understood as 'rogues and toxins', introduced, according to Don Paterson, 'to give the composition a little weight / as rough harmonics do the violin-note / or Pluto, Cheiron and the lesser saints / might do to our lives, for all you know.' Hill likes rough contrasts and perhaps his abstractions sharpen contrast. You can see them like poppies, where 'Poppies, root-torn, blaze into grand remonstrance'.

Some of Hill's famous difficulty, the 'rapid juxtapositions and violent lacunae', are instruments of the 'intelligence at bay'; or ways of expressing in a 'solo polyphony' the 'multi-voiced rumours of the Cave'. The danger is that difficulty becomes mannerism, indulgence and excuse to shirk the demands of organisation and elucidation.

Sensuous and passionate *Odi Barbare* may be, but it is seldom simple, not at any rate to begin with. It is neither a must-have for the poetry novice, nor a suitable starting point for the Geoffrey Hill beginner. He or she would be better advised to study the *Selected Poems* and listen to the Clutag CD of Hill reading in 2006. Nonetheless, *Odi Barbare* may in time come to be seen as among Hill's best. It is placed second in *The Daybooks* sequence. We have already had *Oraclau/ Oracles* (2010) and *Clavics* (2011). Two more — *Al Tempo de' Tremuoti* and *Liber Illustrium Virorum* — are forthcoming in the *Collected Poems: 1952-2012*, due from Oxford University Press next year.

CHOSEN BROADSHEET POET

Richie McCaffery is 25 and a Carnegie scholar at the University of Glasgow, researching the Scottish poets of World War Two towards a Ph.D in Scottish Literature. HappenStance Press recently published his first pamphlet collection of poetry, *Spinning Plates*, and his poems have appeared in many journals and *Salt's Best British Poetry 2012*.

Le voyage dans la lune

By the time the scrap-men took my Dad's car
he had travelled the equivalent of a return
journey to the moon in it, by only commuting
into work forty miles away for ten years.

I think of those spring-heeled astronauts
with their stars and stripes the size of leaves
bringing back samples of lunar dirt and Dad
voyaging just as far, less in space, more in time

discovering nothing but dirty cuffs, each trip
leaving behind as a cairn little pieces of himself.

The Weight

You asked me to move the big bag of compost
from the bottom garden to your new bed.
It had been raining all day the day before
and the bag was heavy, so heavy in fact
it was like changing the date of your dying day,
more luck rolling back a messianic rock.

You shouted from the back door, called me weak
but the bag had taken on so much water.
I think of him sometimes, as you probably do,
lying in his little plot of earth and how
the days when it rains always seem to be
the days when he sags most in the mind.

En piste

In a pub I overheard a drunken butcher
say that the menu had been written
long before the lambs were even born.

In the church I saw figurines of angels
cast in lead as if they were always
destined to fall, anchors to the deep.

I have no free will because of you,
outside the apple tree is in blossom
like something frothing at the mouth.

The Whale

When they burst the swollen stomach
of the washed up dead blue whale
it was like a grenade set off
inside a world-travelled valise
full of souvenirs, all indigestible;
a football, bottles and a piece of rope.

I thought of that gallus passage
in Lewis Grassic Gibbon's *Sunset Song*
where, under the knife, a fat politician's
belly 'fair gushed up with whisky'.
Today I am somehow empty inside,
but eventually will come a great hunger.

NOTES FOR BROADSHEET POETS
Zoe Brigley

reviewing Younger British Poets who all appeared originally in *Agenda*'s online Broadsheets or as chosen young Broadsheet poets in the journal:

Part 2: Social Anatomists

Kathryn Gray: *The Never-Never* (Seren, 2004)
Helen Mort: *A Pint for the Ghost* (Tall Lighthouse, 2009)
Paul Bentley: *Largo* (Smith Doorstop, 2011)
Will Stone: *Drawing in Ash* (Salt)
Omar Sabbagh: *Waxed Mahogany* (Agenda Editions, 2012)
Rebecca Goss: *The Anatomy of Structures* (Flambard 2010)

In the last issue of *Agenda*, I started reviewing some of Britain's neglected younger poets (on the proviso that it is not only the 'young' who are 'breaking into' poetry or producing ground-breaking work). I should add that the term 'neglected' is not meant to undermine the achievements or recognition that these poets have already, but is simply a way of saying that their books and pamphlets deserve more than a 200 word summary in a round-up review.

The first set of poets discussed was made up of 'mythmakers,' poets who engage with cultural or traditional mythologies in order to enhance or subvert them. The second set of poets considered in this, part 2, scrutinize both human and social bodies. These 'social anatomists' are more concerned with examining human motivations and deflating social strictures and the didacticism of our institutions. It is worth reiterating, however, that this category is not meant to reduce the writers' unique personalities. This is not an act of canon-making. The categories are simply a way of organizing a group of diverse voices, and it is perhaps the differences between the writers in each category that are most intriguing.

Kathryn Gray's *The Never-Never* was nominated in 2004 for the T.S. Eliot Prize and the Forward Prize for Best First Collection. Though *The Never-Never* was published some years ago, we include it because when it comes to Gray, the focus is often on her excellent work as an editor (formerly at *The New Welsh Review,* now at Parthian Books). Gray, however, is also an extremely talented poet, who finds inspiration in the South Wales Valleys.

Many of Gray's poems draw on the peculiarities of Welsh working-class culture, but it is also significant that she studied Medievalism at university. Like *Piers Plowman* or *The Canterbury Tales,* Gray's collection focuses on communities of individuals who are presented as pilgrims or wanderers seeking meaning. This might be the significance of the title, which quotes the idiom, to pay something off 'on the never-never'. There is a sense of futility in the phrase, of striving to reach some goal that is unattainable, yet it also might suggest the idea of *carpe diem,* how individuals and communities live for the moment through sex, booze and escapism. In the epigraph, Gray quotes Gothic nineteenth-century poet Ann of Swansea, and throughout *The Never-Never,* Gray conjures a Gothic British neverland of pubs, estates, rainy streets, bedrooms, garages, cafés, and chapels.

These are not empty spaces, however, but places where human beings rub along with one another creating frictions or attractions. The opening poem, 'Joyrider,' compares the 'due disregard' of car thieves with the reactions of those listening to the stolen vehicle roaring through the night. The joyriders impose their presence on middle-class neighbourhoods shattering their cosy existence. Gray teases out the folly of human beings with a wry, knowing sense of humour. So in 'The Italians in the Rain,' Gray describes an unfaithful husband and, turning to his supposedly ignorant wife, she comments, 'it's just possible that she always knew / what he'd done with her best friend and sister'. In this poem and others, the folly depicted often relates to sex. 'A Voyeur's Volume' describes the kitsch sexiness of reading Jackie Collins on holidays, while 'Assignation' sees the narrator and her partner listening to other lovers on the opposite side of a wall.

The romantic encounters, however, are always imagined in the context of a wider world or community. So in 'Meteorology,' a personal, physical act of opening up makes way for the vision of an entire community. Whole vistas open from 'terraced gardens hung with the swings of pegged lines' to 'tarpaulins drawn across a court in Wimbledon'; from 'a lopped half of sun dropped upon an arable land' to 'a yard, tilted right hip, a woman with basket.' The personal act described is inextricable from and constructed by the society and land that acts as a backcloth for the encounter. This link is made explicit in 'The Muse, an Estate,' where the surprise of a romantic encounter is compared to the unexpected turn of 'rundown, loping alleys or the stairwell descents / of some housing estate (their mapped miscellany of food, piss, sex scent).' Nostalgia for past relationships chimes with the reminiscences about spaces and places that are not conventionally beautiful but vital and alive.

The characters and places in *The Never-Never* imbibe what Gray describes in 'Mount Lee' as 'a sense somehow of being late or lost.' This sense of lateness or lostness might apply to the Welsh poet writing in English, a status that Gray interrogates in 'The Pocket Anglo-Welsh Canon.' There is some hope, however, for a race of writers lost to their own tongue because:

> though these words were never ours,
> they will have happened like a history, share the taste
> of copper on the tongue, have a certain easiness
> with human heat

The Never-Never breathes life and warmth into British stereotypes all too easily used in the media. Gray's collection successfully manages to relate personal stories full of the folly and laughter of human pride and endeavour, whilst also conjuring a sense of place and community that is complex, vivid and beautiful.

Like Gray, Helen Mort in *A Pint for the Ghost* seeks to uncover vivid moments of everyday life. Focussing on working-class folk, Mort traverses Northern towns like Bradwell, Chesterfield, Castleton, Derby and Sheffield. Mort refers to Frost, Mackay and Burnside in the collection, all poets who conjure the unspoken histories that haunt places. Her approach is probably best summed up, however, in her poem 'a dram for all the men I've never drunk with,' which sees the narrator drinking with the ghosts of Freud, Byron, Marx and Larkin. These four ghosts do indeed represent different aspects of Mort's poetics which explore Freudian projections of desires, a Byronic Gothic sense of place, a Marxist sense of repressed histories, and a very Larkinesque emphasis on mundaneness and everyday life.

Throughout the collection, Mort uses the space of the public house: 'pubs / where the front door shuts behind you like a coffin lid' ('are you being served?'). Mort developed the poems in *A Pint for the Ghost* as a theatrical show which was performed at the Edinburgh Fringe, and the poem certainly works here as a storytelling vehicle recounting legends, ghostly tales and humourous anecdotes. Often the tales are told with a touch of wry, working-class realism. Take for example 'a pint for true shepherds' when a 'well-fed vicar' brings his sermonizing to the pub, rhapsodising on the role of man as shepherd. A sheep farmer listening to the lecture tells the vicar laconically 'tha know nowt about sheep.'

Disenfranchised workers – pastoral and industrial – are written out of the history books, but they haunt the post-industrial landscapes in Mort's poems. Analepsis allows these ghosts to intrude on the present, so in 'a vodka for the working ghosts,' Mort notes that there are 'shops built where furnaces once breathed' and she conjures the ghosts of 'long-dead steelworkers'. Similarly, in 'a mild for stainless Stephen', there are ghosts 'still sweating from the braziers that vanished years ago'. Particularly eerie is the story in 'full measure for neil moss', which tells of 'the Oxford caver who they lost / in '59.' This ghost story, however, develops beyond being a creepy legend, and becomes instead summoning of the repressed and silenced histories of working people:

> they call to us, from reservoirs
> and mine shafts, long since shut,
> from bricked up wells and tunnel mouth.

Mort presents the repressed workers as figures in limbo unable to free themselves from their oppressed state. When in 'short measure for gabriel hound,' the 'huge shape of a hound' appears to the Bradwell miners, it signals their impending deaths in a mining accident. The workers, however, are heroic and stoic in the face of death, going down 'grim faced, down to the mine / to meet their certain fate'. Altogether, *A Pint for the Ghost* is refreshing in its unabashed focus on working class people, rituals and histories. Mort's characters are vivid and vital, and the haunting images linger, reminding us of the North's rich industrial history.

Like Mort, Paul Bentley is interested in a disenfranchised class of workers in the North of England, but his new pamphlet, *Largo,* focuses specifically on the 1980s miners' strikes. *Largo* uses deeply complex intertextuality to present a personal history and the story of a particular moment and community. The pamphlet is mainly dominated by the long poem, 'The Two Magicians', the title of which refers to the old folk ballad. The ballad tells the story of a blacksmith who pursues an unwilling lady; she escapes by turning herself into different creatures. Finally, she turns herself into a man, and the blacksmith conquers her by turning himself into a woman. It is difficult to tell quite how the symbolism of the ballad tallies with the poem which describes the 1980s miners strikes in Yorkshire. Does the blacksmith chasing the lady represent the Tory pursuit and defeat of the rights of workers? Is the chase bound up with a personal story or is it a tale that sheds light on British society as a whole?

More light is shed by the sequence's two epigraphs, both of which are bound up with a critique of imperialism and conquest. The first is taken from an interview with Margaret Thatcher in which she espouses Victorian values and seems to ignore the interviewer's suggestion that such values create a division of wealth and an unequal society. The second (from Dee Brown's *Bury my Heart at Wounded Knee*) describes Native American chief Sitting Bull's desire to take his people to Canada to the land of his 'grandmother,' Queen Victoria, a plan which, in the light of Victorian imperialist values, is bound to end badly. In addition to these epigraphs, there also appears the alchemical motto, VITRIOL: *Visita Interiora Terrae Rectificando Invenies*

Occultum Lapidem ('Visit the Interior Parts of the Earth; by Rectification Thou Shalt Find the Hidden Stone'). 'The Two Magicians' is then set up as a pursuit of wisdom and the subject to be investigated is British imperialism and the desire for conquest.

Rather than looking at British imperialism abroad, however, Bentley focuses on the Yorkshire miners' strikes of the 1980s and tells the story of how the Northern working-class was conquered by the Thatcher government. The telling of this story is not straightforward, however, and the use of intertextuality is immense. Take for example how each poem is dedicated to a creature: the dove, pike, spider, rabbit, eel, mallard, and fly. We are only given the Latin name and a brief description of every creature from field guides which works as an epigraph for every poem. The use of creatures refers back to the ballad 'The Two Magicians,' where the lady transforms herself into different shapes to escape the blacksmith, but it also has significance in relation to the poems' content. For example, the first poem dedicated to the dove, a romantic symbol, tells a story of unrequited love for a friend's older sister, while the next poem is dedicated to the pike, a creature that resembles the dubious character described: Ripley who is a 'smackhead' and poacher. 'The Two Magicians' is full of authentic characters and voices and even the passages spoken by the chorus ring true, taken as they are from an oral history of the miner's strike.

On the one hand, there are references to cultural texts and figures of the 1980s: Morissey, New Order, Culture Club, the Smiths, Echo and the Bunnymen, the Cure, the magician Paul Daniels, and Arthur Scargill. On the other, the personal stories of growing up in 1980s Yorkshire are elevated by references to Shakespeare, Tennyson, George Herbert and Keats. The use of octets too with inset lines is reminiscent of nineteenth century narrative poetry, though the story told is far less easy to decipher. Keats in particular seems to hold a particular significance with the 'ring-dove frayed and fled' from 'The Eve of Saint Agnes' appearing again and again to signal love unrequited, hopes lost. Near the end of the sequence, the dove is hopeful, however, as its 'Fallen bird seed' offers the possibility of sustenance to the weary miners. Paraphrasing Tennyson's 'The Lotos Eaters,' Bentley imagines the defeated workers like Tennyson's sailors, seeking comfort in oblivion: the 'Waves gushing on an alien shore.' These overpowering waves appear again in the final poem where they are 'Gushing over the pit.' The pieces of Northern culture that remain are explored in the title poem, 'Largo,' and 'Barnsley Abu (a postcard to Paul Muldoon)' which mingle football culture, the popular song and the sublimity of high art to bathetic effect. Altogether, Bentley's *Largo* is uncompromising in its use of intertextuality, which may be a source of irritation for some. This reviewer, however, enjoyed unravelling some of the allusions and layers of the poems, and the result is a far more complex vision of the North.

While the collections reviewed so far have been very much embedded in British culture, Will Stone's second collection, *Drawing in Ash,* has a more European sense of place and community. Like Gray's *The Never-Never, Drawing in Ash* evokes a sense of lateness – of living in an age too late, of discovering an epiphany just before the moment of death, of finding beauty and sublimity in death. Many of the subjects of Stone's poems are historical figures who have some significant role as prophets or philosophers trying to make meaning out of meaninglessness. 'Christ on the Cross – Delacroix' questions Jesus's sacrifice describing the 'Human labour' of the crucifixion:

> ... two wedges hammered down
> no Mary, no mourners, no soldiers
> only bare brown blood-soiled ground

The half-rhyme between 'down' and 'ground' emphasises the act of hammering the two wedges; it is final, desolate and without hope of resurrection. Similarly bleak is 'Nietzsche at the End', which pictures the philosopher after his mental breakdown when he 'wave[s] the world I gnawed white away,' and 'Walser's Last Walk' describes the death of the Swiss writer Robert Walser who, like Nietzsche, suffered a mental breakdown, ending his days in an asylum. 'Chopin in Scotland' describes the composer's final journey before dying in Paris in 1849; Stone describes him as 'an almost leafless branch / bending over the Broadwood.' 'The Clearing' in memory of Walter Benjamin invokes the end of the philosopher's life trying to escape the Nazis, a journey which eventually led to his suicide. In all of these poems, Stone laments the waste and decline of such great men, but also seems to celebrate the intensity of the moment before death, when the world appears with such immense beauty and clarity.

Stone's role as poet is outlined in 'Note Scribbled to the Unsaved' where he addresses those dead before their time, mapping 'every one snuffed out,' 'every fresh heart,' each 'slumped pilot and flak-shredded wings,' and 'suitcases showing through the snow, / un-recovered on a platform.' Stone is a witness to brutality, war and death:

> I have timed my breathing to your
> still rising forms, and have placed
> each of your names in cold churches
> where no one comes.

Many of the poems are memorials and many more are set in burial grounds or cemeteries. In the 'Secret of Picpus Cemetery, Paris,' Stone describes how many victims of Paris's revolutionary Terror were buried there. Imagining the moment before their deaths, Stone invokes 'the cool preamble' of 'the jailer barber's eager shears'. 'In the Ancient Cemetery of Ukkel' uses the overgrown cemetery in Brussels to philosophise about the impermanence of monuments and concludes that 'somewhere two skeletal hands / are waiting for the moment / to release the stilled dove.'

The title poem of the collection 'Drawing in Ash' is based on the testimony of SS officer, Karl Wolff, who was surprised to see Himmler react with revulsion after witnessing the execution of prisoners. Stone cleverly transforms Wolff's act of drawing in ashes to an image that resonates with the outrage of the Holocaust: breathing the ashes of those who died in the gas chambers – drawing in ash. The Holocaust is the subject again in 'The Extinction Plan,' where Stone frames the desire to kill as the inevitable companion of romantic or sexual desire:

> No one wants to be dust.
> No one wants their love left out,
> but nearly every wheel finds the rail
> and follows the tramline to lust.

Selfishness is at the root of modern society in Stone's vision. Everyone wants their own existence and loves to be validated, but that does not stop them from lust or bloodlust, with the image of the rail and tramline presenting eerie echoes of the Jews deported to death camps in World War Two. Violence and lust are twinned again in 'The Antwerp Mannequins,' which explores to the fullest the inevitable comparison between butchery and prostitution:

> [...] all they want is meat, to gnaw the bone
> to tear the haunch and fill
> the emptying barn of their hearts

The prostitutes are meat in a butcher's window to the customers, a familiar metaphor. Yet Stone turns the viewpoint from the voyeur to scrutinize the male customers. They are barns empty of grain, a metaphor which emphasises the hollowness at the heart of those who buy sex, and poses questions about the source of such emptiness. Altogether, *Drawing in Ash* is a striking and poignant piece of work, which strikes at the heart at the problems of modernity. Through telling the deaths of famous individuals like Benjamin, Himmler, Chopin or Nietzsche, Stone raises disturbing questions about civilisation and brutality. Bleak and beautiful, the poems elegise and bear witness, lamenting the emptiness at the heart of Western society.

Bringing a very different sensibility to poetry, Lebanese-British writer Omar Sabbagh considers the social intersections of family, place and community in his sensitive and endearing new collection *Waxed Mahogany*. Sabbagh is a surprisingly prolific writer for a young poet, and has already published two collections: *My Only Ever Oedipal Complaint,* and *The Square Root of Beirut*. Sabbagh's earlier collections celebrated his Lebanese heritage and family, mused on the nature of civilisation, and considered the vagaries of love, in a notorious series of poems to an unrequited lover named C. This new collection develops these themes, reiterating that the personal and social are inextricably linked. The collection begins and ends with quotations from Nabokov's *Pale Fire,* which revolves around the invented poet John Shade, who is arguably an alter-ego for Nabokov. The reference subverts the expectations of the reader. Is the narrator of the poems Sabbagh or a version of Sabbagh, and just how far removed are these versions from the 'real thing'? The epigraph reads: 'I was the shadow of the waxwing slain / by the false azure in the windowpane.' The quotation laments the waxwing's mistake – seeking space and freedom in the reflection in a pane of glass – but it also questions notions of authenticity. The speaker is not the waxwing, but the waxwing's shadow. At the end of the collection, however, when Sabbagh quotes *Pale Fire* again, he signals that the purpose of *Waxed Mahogany* is to recover something of what has been lost: 'I was the smudge of ashen fluff – and I / Lived on, flew on, in the reflected sky.' The feather of the dead bird represents what survives in both real and mirrored worlds.

Similarly, Sabbagh's poems do not merely explore the self – the cult of personality that Nabokov so cleverly subverts – but introduce a cast of characters, many of them real people from Sabbagh's family. Place is also integral to these poems, and Sabbagh continues to list the location where the poem was written beneath the title. These poems are never isolated textual artifacts then, but always embedded in a social context. For Sabbagh, 'Poets, like poems, are pith, are Palestine,' a metaphor that seemingly locates poets and poetry in arenas of revolt, insurgency and upheaval (in 'Palestine'). This is Sabbagh at his most political, yet his main preoccupation in *Waxed Mahogany* is the interconnections between family, lovers and friends – how such connections shape and mould the way in which we view the world. It is no coincidence that in 'A Manned Island,' Sabbagh quotes Donne's maxim: 'No man's an island.'

The first section, 'Of the Licit and the Dear,' is most concerned with family, the title being taken from a poem about his grandfathers whom he never met, but who are described as 'rapid scholars / Of the licit and the dear'. The use of the word 'licit' is interesting, and it is linked in the poem 'The

Band of Brothers' to the task of retaining part of what is lost – the feather of Nabokov's waxwing.

> Stitches for the words, words for the stitches
> For the licit dissection of the river and mist
> That's at the core of what a heart, in its
> Prolonged loudness, misses, missed...

Sabbagh has always been preoccupied with writing about his family, having presented a number of beautiful and poignant poems for his grandmother, mother, and father in earlier collections. What is especially striking in this new collection though, are the complex poems about women through which Sabbagh explores the notion of femininity itself and his own relationship with it. In 'La Veuve' for example, he considers 'a widow busy with her widowhood,' and notes how 'Eyeing her I seem to tug at her'. What emerges from this scrutiny is an astounding litany of beautiful images that unravel what Freud called the 'dark continent' of femininity:

> She wears black: a lewd rhapsody against snow –
> A jeremiad and a passion and a paradox in its folds;
> Something wailing, Pre-Raphaelite, warming, saucing the cold

More explicit examination of womanhood occurs in 'The Feminine,' where the feminine moves from outside the observer to inside: 'That frittering machine within, within, / That lewd racket, that raucous, cloudy din'. In 'Nymph and I,' the epigraph quoting Lacan on the mother reveals a psychoanalytic, philosophical approach to the feminine. Addressing the 'nymph,' the narrator imagines femininity as a greater interconnectedness, a sense of what Freud would call 'oceanic feeling':

> Tell me how all men vanish in you.
> The tall ones and the short ones, the brown,
> and the white, the lacklustre bony
> And the fat treasured ones.
> Tell me your story: we are at sea together
> You and I, unravelled by landfall as yet.

'Nymph and I' has a kind of nostalgia for the connection between mother and child – the state of 'not knowing where I end / and you begin'. This is reiterated again in a poem for Sabbagh's grandmother, 'The Old Pear of Her Body,' where he describes the selflessness of maternity: his grandmother 'Crouching low, making from the old pear / Of her body, a total tender offer'.

The main sequence of the collection, *Waxed Mahogany,* extends this fascination with generosity and unboundedness, but adds a poignant feeling of things lost: that there are limits to how well or how long we can know others. Redemption is still to be found in the feminine, which is what mahogany seems to represent. In '"He",' a poem that begins in self-exploration, Sabbagh turns back to the oceanic, maternal feeling of the feminine: 'Let the polished wood guide us back to our beginnings: / The warm mahogany of burgeon and motherhood'. Whether we can recapture the interconnectedness with our mothers, with the maternal, with the feminine, is questionable, however. In 'His Eyebrows', another poem for his unrequited love C., Sabbagh laments 'What's lost is lost,' and recalling Shakespeare's *Richard III* in 'A Horse, A Horse,' Sabbagh describes the possibility of failure as 'something awry in the corner of a room'; it is 'Something vanishing as a horse; / Something vanishing as horses do.' Sabbagh's antidote for such loss and failure is to commemorate members of his family: his grandfather in 'His Scarf by my Heart'; more poems for his deceased uncle Bisher Faris; and a series of moving poems to his father. The possibilities (or not) of inheritance are explored in 'Sultan,' where Sabbagh describes his father as 'the pulse that wings and sings / and the blood that bleeds in me,' yet the narrator excoriates himself for being 'to him as profane leaf // To mythic tree'. The son can never match his father's greatness, but remains an imprint or shadow.

The sense of loss in familial and romantic relationships is also found in communities and place. So, in the sequence 'Music of the World's Defeat', Sabbagh describes (in the sequence's title poem) how 'we are cusps without feet, fleeting; / That *there is no* measure or meeting / Between the notes, no cause, no ceiling'. Sabbagh locates this feeling of nothingness in the city of Beirut in particular. In '*This* City', he describes Beirut as a 'lame finger triggering / A gun' and 'a struck drum / Which fails to resonate.' Beirut's lack, however, is finally brought back to the context of family and social interaction in 'Split-tongued':

> The deep blues of these locutions,
> My split-tongued family stirs
> A massive, hoary cry in me,
> A huge, dolorous secret,
>
> Like a sea's, say, chief
> Rut, rent, its most choice
> Emotion –

Being dislocated from a single tongue is both painful and generative in

Sabbagh's vision. It creates a lack of permanence, of security, of single and whole identity, but it also brings us back to that sense of oceanic feeling – of being connected to others in a profound and inextricable way. It means existing in a borderland, which echoes the symbolism of the final sequence: 'Lines in the Sand'. Perhaps the most revealing poem in this sequence is 'After Conrad's Preface to *The Nigger of the 'Narcissus'*. Sabbagh completed a PhD at Kings College London on the work of Ford Maddox Ford and Joseph Conrad, and the conclusion to this poem is very Conrad-esque: 'And sense has two meanings: / To make you see and to make you see.' Like Conrad, Sabbagh's poems seeks to evoke sensual experiences, but he is also (as Edmund White labels Ford) a *mythomane*, creating bombastic and hyperbolic images for the love of storytelling. One of Sabbagh's greatest strengths is the beauty and surprise of his images which evoke powerful emotional responses. Take 'In the Hareem', where he describes the inhabitants speaking 'like silken imbeciles, / Distant as bony crickets or khaki crocodiles, / As dry and useless as tardy codicils', or for another example, see 'The Desert of Her' where a kiss is 'lip upon lip like cut wrists'. In painting the self as a series of reactions to people and places, Sabbagh presents a series of poignant and moving poems that transcend the mundane in search of the sublime, the beautiful, the dear and the oceanic. His approach might be summed up by the epigraph to 'De Anima' which quotes Roger Scruton's *The Face of God:* 'The smile of the Mona Lisa is a smear of pigments on a canvas. But the lived world is as real as the Mona Lisa's smile'.

Like Sabbagh, Rebecca Goss is preoccupied with relationships within families, and her new collection *The Anatomy of Structures* deconstructs marriage and relationships in particular. Her poems are disarming; their stories sound anecdotal and personal but the variety of characters and situations involved mean that they can't all be true. The title poem scrutinises human bodies, human memory and the human heart, finding 'historical movement' in 'a new freckle', before turning inwards to map out the 'parts of my heart divided for our children'. The poem and the whole collection represent 'the slow digging out of our histories', and while so many stories end with the 'happily ever after' of betrothal, Goss seeks to uncover 'this new structure of marriage'. The glamour of a grand passion is not the subject of *The Anatomy of Structures,* but instead mundane moments of intimacy and feeling are foregrounded throughout the book.

Goss is preoccupied with observing everyday interactions, while human pain and weakness are often subjects for her poems. So in 'Rise,' a mother allows her child to trace old burns – 'twists / like raw white dough stretching over veins,' and in 'Labor Day, Long Island,' a man watches a loved one's flirtations: how she laughs with another man 'as if she really didn't know / he wanted to touch her.' In 'Jealousy,' a mother witnesses a father/son rivalry so extreme that the father 'Wants the boy to see him being held tight, / fucked into existence' by the boy's mother, and, in 'Her Things,' when a woman asks her boyfriend to remove the toiletries of his ex-lover from the bathroom shelf, she is dismayed to realize that the other woman's 'belongings have morphed / into mine'. Through telling these small, intimate moments, Goss captures the misapprehensions, interactions and frictions in human communities.

The mundane details of these poems are not only powerful but political. In 'Burgle Me', Goss questions the slippage between objectifying women and brutalising them. The woman in the poem is subjected to a burglary during which she is tied up 'like a bound piece of game, / watching them search, empty, steal'. Goss describes how 'one of them leant close, / did something terrible to her eye', an act that secures the right of voyeurism for men only. Flashing forward to months later, Goss describes the woman dancing at a wedding. Moving to the voyeuristic perspective of a male guest, Goss describes how he admired 'the boldness of her pose, / the slit in her skirt' and desires to 'tuck his nails // beneath her eye patch' and 'steal a look'. The victim of the robbery is still objectified by the men who regard her, and the act of making her an object of fantasy is represented as yet another violation.

Goss's poems convey the contradictions and cruelties of human behaviour, as well as vulnerabilities and frailties. This latter feeling is especially redolent in Goss's poems about parents and children. While Sabbagh contemplated parents from the point of view of a son, Goss focuses on parental anxiety about harm coming to one's children which is not often the subject for poetry. Goss conjures a sense of parental helplessness very effectively. In 'Knowledge', a mother imagines her son's suicide as a grown man: how he will be found 'Boots with laces dangling / in a garage, his own children playing outside'. Another mother in 'Growing' describes her husband's guilt when his son's arm is ripped off by an elevator door; she notes that 'We never speak of the blood or the foreign sound // that was my husband screaming'. 'Keeping Houston Time' revolves around parental guilt too, as a mother and father sleep through their son's death in a different time zone. Most poignant is 'Aeroplanes', in which a mother begins to deal with the death of her daughter in a plane accident; she replays the accident, this time imagining herself there able to save her child: 'My hands getting ready to grab the feet, / pull her safely through the trees'. The impossibility of the dream is horrifying and beautiful, and it emphasises the frailty of human hopes. Altogether, *The Anatomy of Structures* is a powerful debut collection that mercilessly scrutinises human follies and weaknesses. Goss's poems about guilty parents, jealous siblings, and mistrustful lovers create a sense of a community of individuals who are helpless on the tides of coincidence and happenstance.

Biographies

Janette Ayachi is a London-born Edinburgh-based poet with a MSc in Creative Writing from Edinburgh University and poetry published in literary print journals such as *Poetry Salzburg Review* and *Gutter*, currently in *Orbis, The Journal, Pushing out The Boa*t and *Southlight #11*, then upcoming in the *The New Writer* and The *Istanbul Review*. She was shortlisted for Write Queer London this year and won the St. Andrews Museum competition set for *StAnza*. Her pamphlet *A Choir of Ghosts* will be published by Red Squirrel press.

R.V. Bailey has published *Course Work* (Culverhay Press, 1997), *Marking Time* (Peterloo Poets, 2004), and T*he Losing Game* (Mariscat Press 2010). For most of her life an academic, she was the extra voice in U A Fanthorpe's poetry readings; together they gave readings throughout the UK and overseas, jointly led poetry courses, and judged a range of poetry competitions. RVB regularly reviews poetry in *Envoi* and other magazines.

William Bedford is an award-winning novelist, children's novelist, poet and short-story writer. His novel *Happiland* was shortlisted for the *Guardian* Fiction Prize. His selected poems, *Collecting Bottle Tops,* and selected short stories and non-fiction, *None of the Cadillacs Was Pink*, were both published in 2009.

Zoe Brigley is an Eric Gregory Award winner. She has had two collections published: *The Secret* (Bloodaxe, 2007) and a new collection, *Conquest* (Bloodaxe, 2012). There was an in-depth interview with her by Peter Carpenter in the Welsh issue of *Agenda*, 'Carpenters of Song' Vol 44, Nos 2-3. Zoe comes from Wales, was a chosen young *Agenda* Broadsheet poet, and is now living in the US.

Gillian Clarke, National Poet for Wales since 2008, is President of Tŷ Newydd, the Writers' Centre in North Wales, which she co-founded in 1990. She was awarded the Queen's Gold medal for Poetry in December 2010, and the Wilfred Owen Award in 2012. Recent books include *A Recipe for Water, At the Source*, and a new collection, *Ice*, published by Carcanet.

Anne Connolly was born in Northern Ireland. She has taught throughout Britain, working more recently as an independent advocate for and with older people in long-term care. Poems have been published in *Horizon, Salt Publishing; Magma; Mslexia; Poetry Scotland; Quarrtsiluni* and *The Tablet*. Her pamphlet, *Downside Up*, was published by *Calder Wood Press* in 2008 and her collection *Love-in-a-mist* (2011) is available at www.redsquirrelpress.com. Anne currently organises the School of Poets at the Scottish Poetry Library.

Tim Cresswell enrolled on the first Faber Academy 'Becoming a Poet' course in 2009 (led by Daljit Nagra), after which he signed up for a PhD in Creative Writing at Royal Holloway, University of London, supervised by Jo Shapcott. He is working towards a first pamphlet collection called *Heft*. He has been published in a variety of magazines including *Poetry Wales, the Rialto, the North* and *Smiths Knoll*. He is a Professor of Cultural Geography at Royal Holloway.

John F. Deane was born on Achill Island, Co. Mayo in 1943 and now lives in Dublin. He is the founder of Poetry Ireland and of the Dedalus Press. He is a major, award-winning poet with several collections to his name, mainly from Carcanet Press. His latest, *The Eye of the Hare*, was published in June 2011 and a new collection from Carcanet is due in 2013. He is a member of Aosdána.

Peggie Gallagher lives in Sligo. Her work has been published widely in Ireland, England and North America. She is a recent winner of the Listowel Poetry Collection prize.

Eamonn Grennan was born in Dublin in 1941 but has lived for many years in Poughkeepsie, New York where he was the Dexter M. Ferry Professor of English at Vassar College until he retired in 2004. He has won many awards and honours and has more than ten collections of poetry to his name. He has also written a book of essays: *Facing the Music: Irish Poetry in the Twentieth Century* (1999). He spends as much time as he can in the West of Ireland.

John A. Griffin was born in Tipperary, Ireland and lived for many years in St. Louis, MO, USA. He holds a BA from St. Louis University and read for his MA and PhD at Washington University, St Louis, where he specialized in German Idealist Philosophy and the work of Samuel Taylor Coleridge. He has had poems published in journals in the US and the UK. John currently lives and works in Riyadh, Saudi Arabia, where he teaches Literature and Directs the English Language Academy for teachers.

Graham Hardie's poetry has been published in *Markings, The Interpreter's House, Gutter, The New Writer, Cake, The David Jones Journal, Cutting Teeth, Nomad* and online at *nth position*. He is 40 and works as a gardener. His latest collection is published by Ettrick Forest Press.

Eleanor Hooker's debut collection of poems *The Shadow Owner's Companion* (Dedalus Press) was published in February 2012. She has a BA (Hons1st) from the Open University, an MA (Hons.) in Cultural History from the University of Northumbria, and an MPhil in Creative Writing (Distinction) from Trinity College, Dublin. She was selected for the Poetry Ireland Introductions Series in 2011. Her poetry has been published in journals in Ireland and the UK. She is a founding member, Vice-Chairperson and PRO for the Dromineer Literary Festival. She is a helm and Press Officer for the Lough Derg RNLI Lifeboat. She began her career as a nurse and midwife.

Rosalind Hudis has had poetry and fiction accepted for publication by a number of journals including *Stand*, the *Interpreter's House* and *The Lampeter Review*. In 2011 she won the Wilfred Owen Bursary and was short-listed for two Cinnamon Press competitions. One of her poems was awarded a commendation in the 2011 National Poetry Competition. She lives near Tregaron, West Wales and is studying for an MA in Creative Writing at Trinity St David's, Lampeter.

Dan MacIsaac spent six seasons working in Canada's North as a prospector, and now lives in Victoria, British Columbia. His poetry has been published in *Pennine Platform, 14, Weyfarers* and *Other Poetry*, and appeared most recently in *Wascana Review*. He has fiction forthcoming in *Stand*. His branch of the MacIsaac clan came from South Uist in the Hebrides and moved in 1792 to Prince Edward Island. There they became established in Rock Barra, before spreading west across the country.

Ann Joyce Mannion lives in Co. Sligo. Her poetry collection *Watching for Signs* was published by Dedalus Press. *Meadbh – The Crimson Path*, a CD of poetry, music and song in collaboration with composer and musician John Carty was released 2011. One of her poems, set to music by Crazy Dog Audio Theatre is included in the *Bee-Loud Glade* anthology published by Dedalus Press in 2011.

Gill McEvoy runs several poetry events in Chester, including workshops under the name *PoemCatchers*. Later this year she will take up her Hawthornden award, and in May 2013 her second collection, *Rise*, will be published by Cinnamon Press. (First collection *The Plucking Shed*, Cinnamon Press 2010). Website: www.poemcatchers.com

Author of the chapbook *Life in Captivity* from Finishing Line Press, **Jennifer A. McGowan** has published in many journals on both sides of the Atlantic, including, most recently, *Acumen* and the *American Journal of Nursing* – the latter being the latest in her line of poetry about being disabled. She holds a PhD in English, and has taught and had her poems used as text at various universities. Her website, with more poetry and examples of her mediaeval calligraphy, can be found at www.jenniferamcgowan.com and on *Agenda*'s online web supplement in tandem with this issue.

W. S. Milne is a Scottish writer living in Surrey. The final part of his poetic trilogy, *Mary Queen o Scots*, was recently published by *Lallans*. He is currently writing a novel.

Mary O'Donnell lives in Co. Kildare, Ireland. She has published six collections of poetry and five works of fiction. Her most recent poetry volume, *The Ark Builders*, appeared in 2009 from Ark Publications, Todmorden. She was recently writer-in-residence at the Centre Culturel Irlandais in Paris. She is a member of the Irish inter-disciplinary peer-elected arts organisation, Aosdana.

Liam Ó Muirthile is from Cork, Ireland. His latest collection, *An Fuioll Feá / Woodcuttings – New and Selected Poems*, is to be published by Cois Life in February 2013.

Mandy Pannett works as a free lance creative writing tutor. She has won prizes and been placed in competitions and her poetry has been published in international journals and anthologies. Recent work has been translated into German and Romanian. She has also acted as selecting editor for *South* and been a judge of national poetry competitions. She has had three poetry collections published: *Bee Purple, Frost Hollow* (Oversteps Books) and *Allotments in the Orbital* (Searle Publishing) Her novella, *The Onion Stone*, was published in November 2011 by Pewter Rose Press.

Sheenagh Pugh was born in 1950 and read German and Russian at Bristol. She has published many collections of poems with Seren, the latest being *Long-Haul Travellers* (2008) and *Later Selected Poems* (2009). She is working on a new collection to be published in 2013. She is Welsh and Irish by descent and lived many years in Wales, but now lives in Shetland.

Ed Reiss lives and works in Bradford. He has written *The Strategic Defence Initiative* (Cambridge University Press, 1992); *Marx: a Clear Guide* (Pluto Press, 1997); and *Your sort*, which was shortlisted for the Aldeburgh First Collection Award, 2011.

Gabriel Rosenstock is a poet, novelist, playwright, author/translator of over 160 books, mostly in Irish. He taught haiku at the Schule für Dichtung (Poetry Academy) in Vienna. He also writes for children. Among the anthologies in which he is represented are *Best European Fiction* 2012 (Dalkey Archive Press, USA). His recent comic novel is called, *My Head is Missing*.

Lorna Sherry completed her degree at Bangor, Wales, in 2006. Now, with poetry and reviews accepted by, *Orbis, Skald, Shop, Envoi*, and the anthology *The Lie of the Land* (Cinnamon Press), Lorna is once again at home on the Isle of Arran, Scotland.

Robert Stein's poems have appeared in *Agenda* as well as in *Poetry Review, The Wolf, Ambit, Magma, The Rialto, Poetry Wales* and *Envoi*. He lives in London and reviews contemporary classical music for *Tempo* and *International Record Review*. *The Very End of Air*, his first collection, was published by Oversteps Books in 2011.

TEAR–OFF SUBSCRIPTION FORM

Pay by cheque (payable to 'Agenda'), or
Visa / MasterCard

SUBSCRIPTION RATES ON INSIDE FRONT COVER

1 Subscription (1 year) =
- 2 double issues
- 1 double, 2 single issues
- or
- 4 single issues
- (The above is variable)

Please print

Name: ....

Address: ....

....

....

.... Postcode ....

Tel: ....

Email: ....

Visa / MasterCard No: ☐☐☐☐ – ☐☐☐☐ – ☐☐☐☐ – ☐☐☐☐

Expiry date: ☐☐ – ☐☐

Please tick box:

    New Subscription ☐   Renewed Subscription ☐

    (or subscribe online – www.agendapoetry.co.uk)

Send to: AGENDA, The Wheelwrights, Fletching Street, Mayfield,
East Sussex, TN20 6TL
Tel: 01435-873703

NEW COLLECTION FROM clutag / AGENDA EDITIONS

Rodin's Shadow: Patricia McCarthy

Rodin's Shadow
Patricia McCarthy

'*Rodin's Shadow* is a tour de force with its impressive energy, and the almost uncanny smell of the real that it gives off. And these women are real, that's for sure. I love the way the sections feed off each other and there's a powerful sense of accrual. There are changes in pace, changes in tempo, twists in diction, all of which ensure that the register is up, the momentum brightening; they never threaten the unity of the whole piece, however, and this makes for a page-turner. A highly ambitious, highly original and achieved book, full of passionate endeavour.'   Tim Liardet

'This collection is truly moving. The poems are energetic, exciting, demanding and rewarding. Patricia McCarthy is doing something unique here, using persona and art history to great effect. There is an energy to the language, and a half-wild experimentation that is uplifting and yet controlled. The shifting between rhyme and free verse is also exact and exacting. There is a fine labour manifest throughout and I find the whole a rich achievement.'
John F. Deane

'I am struck by the poignancy of this collection and particularly like the sense of place in many of the poems which pull off the rare trick of being deeply personal yet, through Patricia McCarthy's deft poetic skill – the ethereal imagery, the subtle use of rhyme and line foregrounding – become at the same time universal. This collection is a tour de force, so assured poetically and dramatically. Sensual, atmospheric, engaging, highly moving at the end, with a wonderful sense of narrative drive, the work is of a consistently high quality.'
Josephine Balmer.

'Hats off to *Rodin's Shadow*. It is excellent: intense, oneiric, erotic, very poetic, very passionate, and deeply knowledgeable about its characters and background. An exhausting but thoroughly enjoyable exploration of the psychic territory of those brilliant, destroyed women. There is so much behind the writing, and there isn't a single dud poem here.'
Tony Roberts

'These poems take Camille Claudel, Gwen John and Rose Beuret as starting points and muses, spinning out from their stories and emotions beautiful, lyrical poems, sometimes in an elegiac tone, sometimes even flooded with tragedy and regret, but also with a visceral, muscular hold on everyday reality, physical, outspoken and sustained through Patricia McCarthy's inimitable, elegant style and polish.'
Sue Roe

Price £10 plus £1.50 p&p.

Order from:
Agenda, The Wheelwrights, Fletching Street, Mayfield, East Sussex TN20 6TL
Tel 01435 873703 or from the online bookshop www.agendapoetry.co.uk

TWO NEW COLLECTIONS FROM AGENDA EDITIONS

by former young *Agenda* Broadsheet Poets: Caroline Clark and Omar Sabbagh

Saying Yes In Russian

"We breathe a sea-thawed air from a sea that isn't there." – Caroline Clark's collection explores the Russia she knows intimately – city, forest, snow – and always with a music that seems to soothe the fear of gaps she finds, edges beyond the edge. Clark's poems have a serenity, a beauty, that knows what perhaps the best lyric knows: "weightlessness takes the strain."

Richard Price, author of Lucky Day

In this compelling first collection, Caroline Clark plays with languages and with language itself. Her vision is pure and touched with the numinous. Her poems, delicate yet strong, at times impressionistic, catch different lights, essences, tastes and colours – all laid on carefully with a palette knife. Through time and place she leads the reader to the centre of things in a sure, promising voice totally her own. W.S. Milne

£8.50 plus £1.50 p&p

Waxed Mahogany

'Sabbagh is a rare and gifted poet. He brings enormous pressure to bear on his themes – love, existential meaning, the rage against darkness, an identity finely tuned to both Beirut and the West – marshalling philosophy and literary allusion with intelligence and elegance so that the reader is immersed in his distinctive world in which '…sense has two meanings: / To make you see and to make you see.' (After Conrad's Preface…). Waxed Mahogany has the hallmarks of his previous two collections – an emotional intensity and vivid honesty in constant dialogue with the metaphysical and analytical – but with an increasingly assured voice and daring range; an extraordinary and exciting poet.'   Dr Jan Fortune, Editor, Cinnamon Press & Envoi

'In Waxed Mahoghany you will find poems written by an audacious young poet that cover the topics most young poets write on: parents, elegies, lust and longing, mortality; but unlike many published today, you will not find ordinary language in any of them. Perhaps it comes from Sabbagh's dual identity as Arab and Englishman, but one hears echoes of Mahmoud Darwish, Nizar Qabbani, Fady Joudah in the poems' alliterations, bold rhymes, surprising metaphors, richness in noun and verb. Sabbagh writes with a refreshing, muscular formalism to challenge the pallid 'free verse' so much in vogue. A winner.'

Norbert Hirschhorn, MD, author of Monastery Of The Moon

£9 plus £1.50 p&p

Order from:
Agenda, The Wheelwrights, Fletching Street, Mayfield, East Sussex TN20 6TL
Tel 01435 873703 or from the online bookshop www.agendapoetry.co.uk

Visit the website www.agendapoetry.co.uk

- **New web supplement to this issue**
- **Poems, essays, reviews, artwork**
- **Special feature:** Medieval Celtic calligraphy by Jennifer A. McGowan

Poems:
Eamonn Grennan
Adam Elgar
Alice Pickering
Angela Topping
Atar Hadari
Daniel King
Emma Lee
Jennifer McGowan
John Gladwell
Sheila Hamlton
Lorna Sherry
Mandy Pannett
Marek Urbanowitz
Martin W. Bennett
Matthew Rhodes
Melinda Lovell
Peter Branson
Rosalind Hudis
Sally Festing
Stuart Medland
William Francis

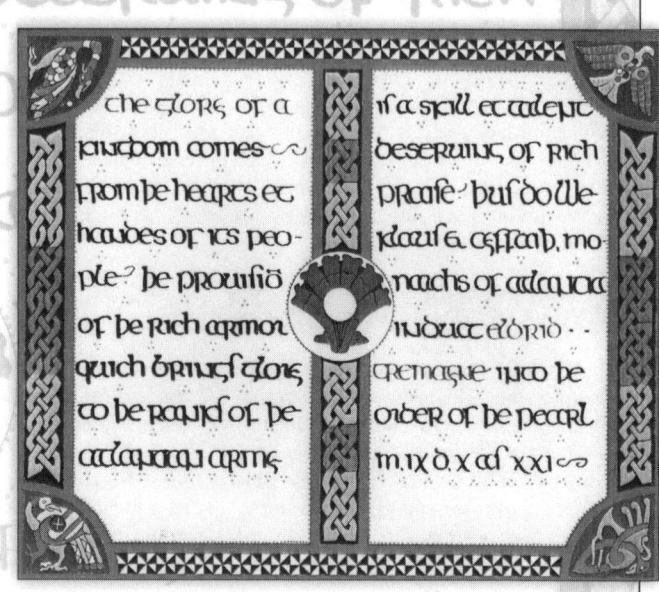

Essays/reviews:
Derek Mahon on Patrick MacDonogh
Gabriel Rosenstock on The Irish Language and its Literature
Adam Wyeth on Desmond O'Grady
Anne Marie Connolly: The Poetry Pamphlet in Scotland
Wendy Holborow on Tegwen Lewis: Neglected Welsh Poet
Omar Sabbagh on Zoe Brigley

SUPPORT AGENDA BY GIVING THE PRESENT OF
A SUBSCRIPTION TO A FRIEND
Simply fill in the form overleaf and send it off, or subscribe online.